AuthorHouse™
1663 Liberty Drive, Suite 200
Bloomington, IN 47403
www.authorhouse.com
Phone: 1-800-839-8640

First published by AuthorHouse 8/26/2008

ISBN: 978-1-4343-6619-1 (sc)

Library of Congress Control Number: 2008905160

Printed in the United States of America
Bloomington, Indiana

This book is printed on acid-free paper.

RACING FOR THE GOLD

THE STORY OF LYLE SHELTON AND THE RARE BEAR

Dell Rourk

authorHOUSE®

To the late Birch Matthews who encouraged me to write the story of the young aviator who built and raced his own airplane in pursuit of speed in the air; to my late husband Hersch, who tolerated far too many frozen dinners and burned biscuits during the years of research and writing; and to Lyle Shelton, whose motto was "fly fast and turn left" for over thirty years --- thank you for your friendship, love and support!

"There is no excuse for an airplane unless it will fly fast".

Roscoe Turner

PROLOGUE

The pleasant hum of conversation hovered over the large group of men and women as they moved about the spacious Samuel P. Langley Theater at the National Air and Space Museum in Washington, D.C. At the front of the room heavy curtains framed a movie screen showing the winged logo of the National Aeronautic Association. On the narrow stage before the screen ranged a few chairs for dignitaries and the podium for the master of ceremonies. There was an air of anticipation among the diverse group---young, old, civilian, military --- as they awaited the beginning of the National Aeronautic Association awards ceremony which would recognize some of these individuals for their outstanding accomplishments in the aviation field. Among them stood a tall, lean man who spoke with a soft drawl that marked his West Texas background. He stood erect, hands on hips, hazel eyes looking directly at his listener as he answered questions about himself and his partner --- an airplane named *Rare Bear*. It was March 11, 1996, and Lyle Shelton was here to receive the prestigious Pulitzer Trophy in Aviation for his unequaled records and contributions to Unlimited air racing.

When his name and achievements were announced Lyle stood at the podium to quietly praise the many people who had helped him over the years with their expertise, talents, and material contributions. He told his audience he was living his childhood dream to "fly fast". And, he promised, he would continue---with help---to fly even faster in his amazing Bearcat.

Following World War I Ralph Pulitzer, an American newspaper publisher, established an award for pylon air racers to encourage aircraft designers and manufacturers to look for improvements leading to faster speeds. Both the United States Army and Navy were interested in developing better performance aircraft. They allocated funds to design faster, more powerful planes that they then entered in the Pulitzer race. The first Pulitzer race was held November 17, 1920, starting at Mitchell Field, Long Island. Thirty-seven racers took off individually and were timed separately over the twenty-nine mile triangular closed course for four laps. Army Captain C.C. Moseley won the event flying a specially built Verville-Packard aircraft at an average speed of 154.5 mph/248.6 kph. The series was discontinued six years later after the 1925 race. Average speeds in pylon air racing in the original six-year period increased from 156.5 mph to 248.9 mph. The award was re-activated in 1991 to recognize the modern day records and record holders.

Lyle first raced the airplane he had rebuilt and modified from a wrecked F8F-2 Grumman Bearcat in the 1969 Reno National Championship Air Races. By 1995 he and the Bearcat had established a new 3-km world speed record., 528.329 mph, for piston-engine propeller-driven aircraft. They also set a new Time-to-Climb record of 3,000 meters in 91.9 seconds. They dominated the Unlimited air-racing scene between 1973 and 1996 with new qualifying speeds and Gold race wins as Lyle continued to modify and improve the performance of the Bearcat. He was, and still is, an entertaining speaker before diverse groups such as elementary school students, air race fans, or aviation company employees. He adopted the motto "Fly Fast".

As Lyle relaxed in his hotel room later that evening he reminisced back through the years that led him to this honor---back to his childhood in West Texas.

CONTENTS

01

THE EARLY YEARS

His birth date is listed as June 15, 1933, but Lyle Shelton jokes, "I was never born, just gradually accumulated during a sandstorm in the middle of a tumbleweed one night and blew up against Miz Shelton's back door. I went 'waaah, waaah, waaah' and Miz Shelton picked me up and took me in. I asked for whiskey. She gave me warm milk. I got my first crop dusting job when I was six months old. Been flying airplanes ever since."

Lyle was born at his grandparents' house in Brownfield, Texas but lived his first six years in the village of Tokio, population approximately fifty people, about 18 miles west of Brownfield. His mother, Ida Mae, and father, Joe, operated a combination country grocery store, Magnolia gas station and the local post office.

Lyle's grandfather owned a half section farm with a store on one corner, a little red brick school house—maybe four rooms—on another corner. The Sheltons lived in the back of the store. It was somewhat primitive for the time. There was no running water, indoor plumbing, or flushing toilets. The family (and visitors) used a little two-seater wooden outhouse behind the store.

During the 1930s the United States was suffering from a terrible drought and depression. The West Texas countryside was dry and sandy with skies darkened by towering clouds of gritty dust rolling from the east across the fields and towns. Lyle's Mother used wet sheets at night to cover him and his sister to keep them from inhaling the polluted air during the frequent sandstorms. During the day the two children played in the dusty open field next door to their Dad's store. They watched as old worn-out cars and trucks jammed with grim-faced men and women, their listless children, and elderly family members rolled by. The vehicles were piled high with mattresses, chickens, furniture—everything the families could carry away from their now abandoned farms. They were hungry and they were homeless.

Every week there were more people—some called them 'Okies'--- traveling from the deserted, barren fields of the southwestern states of Oklahoma, Arkansas and Texas on their way to California towns like Bakersfield and Fresno or to the cotton and grain fields in the San Joaquin valley trying to find work. Some made their way to the Pacific coast town of Monterey to find jobs in the fish canneries. The weary, sad-looking children weren't smiling or waving at the two Shelton youngsters playing in the dry, torrid fields beside the road. They rode stony-faced, desperately wishing for this journey to end soon.

Young as he was, Lyle sadly remembered those days. "When I read John Steinbeck's *Grapes of Wrath* the scenes of despondent people seeking jobs and food were real. I saw it happening. I'll never forget them."

The Tokio residents complained about the grooves worn wheel rims of dilapidated old cars and trucks were carving into their newly paved road built by the Works Progress Administration. The travelers who stopped at the store complained when they had to use the outhouse, muttering that the Sheltons were denying them the use of a 'real' bathroom.

Lyle commented, "That's all we had. It's what we used. There were no flushing toilets in the little wind-blown community of Tokio."

There were not many pre-school age children around the small village. Comic books sold in his parents' store included Lyle's favorite *Smilin' Jack Martin*. The handsome pilot-hero wore a cool leather helmet and a dashing white scarf as he flew from one island to another with his Hawaiian side-kick 'Fat Stuff'. They out-flew, outsmarted, and outfought villains with names like 'The Claw', 'The Head', or 'Toemain the Terrible' who were committing terrible deeds. Gorgeous, curvaceous 'de-icers' were ever present to lavish smiles and praise on Smilin' Jack and 'Fat Stuff". Fantasy inspiring adventures for a lonely four-year-old Texas boy.

No wonder Lyle's first role model was a pilot. For Christmas that year his favorite present was a leather aviator's helmet and scarf like the one worn by Smilin' Jack.

Movie matinees and newsreels featured daredevil, barnstorming pilots; however, not many airplanes strayed into the Brownfield area. Lyle's parents thought it would be fun for him to see one up close and go for his first ride. While visiting relatives in Waco, Texas they took Lyle to the local airport where a few tail-draggers belonging to nearby ranchers and crop-dusters were parked. His Dad arranged with a local pilot for their first airplane ride. It was unforgettable. He and his Dad climbed into the front seat of a Waco cabin plane. He sat on his Dad's lap intently watching everything the pilot did.

He said. "As we taxied to the runway I watched the spinning prop and listened to the engine getting louder and louder. The powerful engine was vibrating; I was so excited. There was a short pause at the end of the runway, then a lurch and we were racing down the tarmac. The engine roared so loud."

The pilot flew around the Brownfield/Tokio area with Lyle and his Dad looking down on the houses, cars, and fields. Everything looked so different—not real. They could see trees and roads and buildings, but they were not really sure where they were without the pilot's help to identify the landscape below them. The flight was over too soon. They floated down towards the runway, bumped a couple times, then slowed and swung a wide curve. A short taxi ride, then they stopped in front of the hangar. Lyle wanted to go flying almost every day after that flight, but it was a lot of years before those wishes came true.

Later that year Mrs. Shelton's sister Evelyn and her husband John L. Cruce took Lyle with them to the Fair Park fairgrounds near the Cotton Bowl in Dallas.

He described his favorite carnival ride, "You sit in this little cylindrical thing simulating an airplane and it rolls around and it swings around and boy, I just had a whale of a time. I would not get out of that contraption. I used up all of John L's quarters, or whatever it cost to ride it. I did enjoy getting upside down and rolling around and playing. They could hardly pull me away from that ride. I really felt I was in an airplane. I wanted to do it forever."

The Sheltons moved to Brownfield, Texas when Lyle was six years old and entered elementary school. Lyle's Mother, Ida Mae, was from a family of fourteen children. Some had died young but by 1940 there were still eight sisters and one brother in the area. A lot of cousins were classmates at school. Mrs Shelton described Lyle as "active, quiet, somewhat shy, happy, and popular". Brownfield became his home base. He would return there often in later years to relax within this strong family group.

Lyle was eight-years old when WWII began and his Uncle John went into the Army. His Aunt Evelyn hired Lyle to help Saturdays and after school at Cruce Auto Parts store while Uncle John served in the Pacific. Sometimes he waited on customers at the front desk but his main job was keeping the boxes and parts dusted off, keeping the inventory straight, unloading and moving inventory around. His Aunt Evelyn let him work on some engines so he learned about internal combustion engines early on.

Adjacent to Cruce Auto Parts was Harris Machine Shop. Lyle could go out the back door of the auto parts store, walk a few steps and go into the back door of the machine shop to visit Mr. Harris. His curiosity about how engines worked, what they did, and how to improve their performance continued throughout his life leading him to challenge and question engineers in various fields from aerodynamics to the special fuels.

Of course it was not all work for Lyle. He was almost six feet tall, slender and quick to smile when he entered Brownfield High School. He played the trumpet in the school band, and was fascinated by boxing. He was a regular reader of *Ring* magazine. A punching bag in the school gym gave him a chance to practice technique he read about in the magazine. The gymnasium was open several evenings a week to adults and students to exercise. Some of the men there had training and experience in the boxing ring. They gave Lyle some informal instruction; however, he needed an experienced boxing coach to train him for competition. None was available. Years later Lyle wanted to join the Navy's boxing program. He chuckled when he recalled that the Navy did not allow officers to participate in the program. They thought the enlisted men would do everything they could to 'kick ass' when up against an officer.

Sometime after the end of WW II Roy Harris and his son Pete established a Fixed Base Operation at Brownfield Airport. It was a small dirt strip south of town, not the airport of today. Roy and Pete maintained a crop dusting service, operated a flight school, and serviced general aviation aircraft. Pete had been in the Army Air Corps during the war flying reconnaissance aircraft in the China, Burma, India theater of operations. He was a modest, medium height freckle-faced man who looked nothing at all like Smilin'Jack. But Pete had lots of stories to tell about 'flying the hump'.

Lyle and his buddies started hanging around the Harris's FBO cleaning and waxing airplanes in exchange for airplane rides. They loved to gather around to listen to Harris's slow Texas drawl as he recounted his experiences flying reconnaissance in the rugged CBI theater of war. Lyle jokes with Harris these days that he is still owed a ride or two for some of the airplane waxing he had done.

"Pete was going to give me flight time but we never got around to it. I was involved in school, boxing, trombone and piano lessons, a girlfriend or two, and did not have enough money left to take real flying lessons."

Lyle delayed his flying ambitions while he finished high school and college.

In 1950, after graduating from high school, Lyle gave serious thought to his future. He spent hours in the library reading about different branches in the engineering field.

He recalls, "I saw a movie with John Wayne where he was a mining engineer in South America. Wayne was smart, sure and hardy, and he was always right. He ended up marrying the General's daughter."

Mining seemed like an adventurous field so in the fall of 1950 he enrolled in the Mining Engineering program at Texas Western College, (formerly Texas College of Mines), now known at Texas-El Paso (UTEP).

After his freshman year he and four classmates signed up with the Colorado School of Mines for six weeks of practical experience in a working mine. They went to Bingham Canyon, Utah, just southwest of Salt Lake City where the big open pit mine is located to work in a large lead-zinc mine. One day in early August Lyle was working the face of a stope, about fifty feet down in the shaft, drilling holes, tamping and filling them with dynamite, when a big rock slab fell on him, knocked him down into a sitting position.

"I reached over to get my hard hat and put it back on when another big slab fell from the roof and hit my back driving my head down between my knees. The other guys dug me out, got some help, then they put me in a basket and pulled me up and out of the shaft."

Lyle was taken to Holy Cross Hospital in Salt Lake City. He had a split vertebra, stayed in the hospital two weeks, then they put a cast on him and he flew home in a United DC6B.

" It was my first commercial airplane flight. The DC6-B was the latest and greatest of airliners at that time. I thought the stewardesses were really nice, too."

He wore the cast for four months during the next semester of college. He worked out in the gym to build up his strength and was doing some boxing with the Catholic Youth Organization when he entered the Golden Gloves tournament in the welter-weight division. He was the favorite to win until his opponent came over the top with an overhand right. He caught Lyle and knocked him cold. Lyle decided to make boxing a hobby.

Mining was not as rewarding for Lyle as it had been for John Wayne's character in the movie. Several of his relatives were working in the oil fields of West Texas at that time. They encouraged him to switch to something in the oil industry. His roommate had decided to transfer to Texas Tech in Lubbock, closer to Lyle's home. In January they both enrolled at Texas Tech where he began to study Petroleum Engineering.

During the next summer vacations they worked in the oil fields. In 1952 and 1953 he was a 'roughneck'. He worked for a widely known boss-toolpusher, W. D. 'Haywire' Brown. In the summer of 1954 he worked as a 'roustabout' in an oil field near Maljamar, New Mexico. (A 'roughneck' works on the drilling rig when you are drilling'; a 'roustabout' works on production after wells are drilled, servicing wells, etc.) . This was hard physical labor. They worked in extreme heat, dirt, balky machinery, and toughened veterans of the oil fields. He ended hot, sweaty days with aching muscles, sun burn, and a sore back. Social life in the oil fields was a few beers with the guys at the local beer halls. The pay was OK. Still, when he graduated in June, 1955, with a Bachelor of Science degree in Petroleum Engineering, he wondered what was in his future. He didn't know Uncle Sam had plans for him. His life was about to take a radical change of direction.

02

The Navy Years

After graduation the draft board informed Lyle because he was single it would not be long before he would be called for duty. There was a 'cease fire' in the Korean conflict; however, the military was still remaining at almost full strength. It was his opportunity to learn to fly! He applied for the Navy aviation officers candidate program with visions of streaking through the skies in powerful Navy jets. He reported to Buckley Naval Air Station in Denver, Colorado for a battery of tests and a physical examination, was accepted for pre-flight training. On March 25, 1956 he reported to historic Pensacola Naval Air Station in Florida. Instead of the stark, parched fields of West Texas and New Mexico Lyle now adjusted to the lush tropical heat and humidity of the Gulf Coast. He could see fishing trawlers as they chugged out towards the Gulf of Mexico, riding high on the water as they left port, hoping to return low and loaded with fish.

He spent his first year in basic training at Whiting Field in T-34s. Lyle and his classmates didn't go straight out to the field and hop into an airplane with an instructor and learn to fly. Not every student who reported in knew exactly how an airplane can fly. They had to learn the parts of the airplane and why each part was needed to make the aircraft get off the ground and stay in the air. They were soon adding new words to their conversations: ailerons, flaps, trim tabs, vertical stabilizer, horizontal stabilizer, rudder, elevator, thrust, lift, drag, roll, pitch, and gravity. Inside the cockpit they were facing a panel of dials and gauges reporting crucial engine information: manifold pressure, altimeter, fuel indicator, engine temperature, heading indicator, turn and bank indicator, rate of climb, and more engine gauges to keep them in touch with their machine. To guide them in the air corridors they learned to read the 'charts'—topographical maps looking down at the landscape below them indicating freeways, roads, railroads, towns and cities, airports, elevations of hills and mountains. There were weather charts to study. They had to recognize the significance of towering black clouds and puffy white ones. Some of his classmates wanted to fly an airplane but were not willing to put so much time into studying engines, weather, and map reading. A few did dropout. Lyle loved it. He loved learning and he loved learning everything he could to be a better pilot.

The Navy also made sure the students knew and observed FAA and military regulations. Military discipline and uniform regulations were strictly judged. Soon the disparate group of strangers became classmates and friends. In July, 1956, after four months pre-flight training Lyle was commissioned an ensign. (If you had a college degree you were commissioned after four months. If you didn't have your degree the student was commissioned after eighteen months, when he finished flight training.)

Formation and instrument flying reminded Lyle how far aviation had advanced since Pete Harris flew his light spotter plane into the war zone about fifteen years earlier.

When training ended at Cory Field Lyle eagerly looked forward to the next phase---gunnery and carrier qualifications to take place at Barrin Field in Alabama. He was now flying SNJs, the Navy's version of the Army's T-6 Texan basic training airplane. A mock-up of a carrier deck was marked out on a section of runway where the students began practicing for take-offs and landings from an actual carrier deck. It was about a year, at the end of basic training, when the students flew out to the carrier Antietam, a WWII carrier of the Essex class, to do the required six carrier landings. The Navy was still 'flying the paddles' during landings. (Picture a man stationed on one side of the deck communicating with the pilot by radio and signaling him with two over-sized, colorful table tennis paddles that he is too high or too low or off center for landing.)

Lyle made his six straight landings without a wave-off, the only one in the class to do so.

"Wave-offs? Sometimes you knew why, sometimes you didn't know why. You could fly a good pass and get a wave-off. When you got a wave-off, the deal was you'd go around. You didn't ask any questions. The LSO (Landing Signal Officer) from your squadron debriefed your landings and marked you down. It was a necessary part of training for proficiency. I think I was so motivated and liked to be in airplanes so much that I was relaxed and confident. I think I enjoy flying more than most people."

At their next station---the Naval Aviation Air Station in Corpus Christi, Texas--- the students met their toughest course. They faced fifty hours of instrument training, most of it inside the cockpit under the hood---and not everyone made it. Lyle thought it the hardest part of his training, so far. He spent long hours studying. It was a great day when he jumped out of the simulator after the final session.

Students transitioned to the AD Skyraiders for six months of advanced training. They chose patrol, anti-submarine, or fighter or light attack duty. Lyle had seen a "big ole AD" at Cadmus Field, and thought he would like to fly ground attack. He requested that and got it. The ADs (Able Dogs) were the last of the piston powered propeller driven carrier planes. They had an exciting mission: lots of dive bombing, rockets, strafing, and low level flying. The tall Texas boy was eager to try it.

While with Air Group One Lyle flew his first jet, an FJ3 Fury, the Navy's tailhook version of the Air Force F-86. The commanding officer of the squadron next door and his own commanding officer let the Skyraider pilots fly jets and the jet pilots fly Skyraiders on their vacations and holidays. Lyle didn't miss any opportunity to fly another new type of aircraft.

After graduation from advanced training at Corpus Christi, TX, he was assigned to Attack Squadron Fifteen (VA-15) in Air Group One attached to the carrier FDR out of Mayport, Florida, as part of the Second Fleet. They flew their airplanes to Mayport where the planes were hoisted aboard the carrier. For several months they were basically attached to and flew out of NAS Jacksonville. They became proficient flying off the carrier deck, landing at Jacksonville, then returning to land on the carrier. They did their carrier qualifications, deployments to Guantanamo Bay and up and down the East Coast.

"Sometimes we'd land on the deck while the ship was at sea and do some training….take-offs and landings. It was challenging at first."

There were a lot of excited crewmen and new pilots as the carrier sailed eastward across the Atlantic Ocean, through the Straits of Gibraltar, then across the Mediterranean to Naples, Italy. It continued up the Italian coast, stopped offshore by Genoa, then continued down the coast to Pisa, Nice, Cannes and into Barcelona, Spain. At each stop Lyle and his buddies went ashore to sight-see, sample the local food and inspect the local bars. There were mixed responses to their visits. Some of the young sailors did not like the food, some chafed at the locals who didn't understand English. There were a few who went straight to the bars and got no further until they staggered back aboard their carrier. Lyle found he didn't care for all the food. He liked his Texas beef. He did enjoy sight-seeing and meeting the townspeople.

In January 1959, Lyle was promoted to Flight Officer. He was responsible for scheduling all squadron flying and coordinating flight training. He kept flight and training records and statistics for the pilots and aircraft. He earned three Navy 'E' awards for pilot proficiency in various competitive exercises.

Lyle loved the flying but didn't like the administrative duties that went with his rank as Lieutenant (Junior Grade). He left the Navy in November 1959 when he received orders to go to a squadron he didn't want to go to. He returned to Texas where he married his high-school girlfriend and went to work for an oil company. Within the year the oil company went broke, he discovered the marriage was a mistake and the marriage ended. Lyle missed the flying and travel. He did not want to go back to the oil or mining industries. He contacted the Navy Bureau of Personnel and told them he wanted to come back in the Navy and he wanted to fly jets. They offered to make him an instructor in T2J jet trainers at Meridian, Mississippi.

While waiting for a reporting date Lyle went to work with R. L. McKenzie crop dusting in the Texas panhandle near Pampa. He spent about six weeks in the wheat fields spraying green bugs. It was his first crop dusting job.

"That's where I met Lefty Gardner. He had the fanciest Stearmans in the whole state of Texas. He fixed them up with razor back headrests. Years later, when I met him again at Reno, he did not remember that meeting but I sure did. Lefty was a big name among Texas crop dusters."

In 1963, after two years as a T2J jet instructor at Meridian Lyle was posted to Randolph Field, Texas for the officer exchange program with the United States Air Force. His students were experienced, top rated pilots going through their instructor checkouts. They came from every Air Force command and compared problems being experienced with the various airplanes each was currently flying. They discussed how to solve unusual and challenging situations. Quick-thinking actions in an emergency would be based on what they learned in these classes. Lyle felt he himself had also learned a lot about handling an airplane in unusual attitudes. It was knowledge he drew upon in later years as an air race pilot.

03

A New Dream

In the fall of 1964 Lyle's temporary tour with the Air Force ended. He would be leaving Randolph Field soon so he decided to take a thirty-day leave, hop Navy flights to foreign ports, and see the world. He wanted to explore different countries, sample exotic foods, listen to foreign languages spoken around him as he sipped coffee in sidewalk cafes. He planned to visit Hawaii, Japan, maybe Hong Kong and Shanghai, India, possibly Australia. This was a difficult period for Lyle. He was restless. He still wanted to be in the air and flying. The probability was his next promotion would involve less flying and more administrative work. When he returned from his leave it would be time for him to ask for his next assignment.

He flew the first leg of his journey in a C-54 with the chief of staff of the Belgium Air Force. Their destination was Hamilton Field, the picturesque U.S. Air Force base about twenty-five miles north of San Francisco, California.

The first evening, dressed in his Navy whites, he went to the Hamilton Field Officers Club. A group of Air Force pilot friends from Reese's Air Force base had flown in during the day in T-38 jet trainers and were spending the night at Hamilton. Lyle recognized several he had checked out or instructed at Randolph Field during the past year.

He sheepishly remembers that night. "We got together and went into town, met some girls, raised hell and I don't know where we all ended up but I woke up in a flower bed the next morning with a fly walking down my nose and the sun coming up over the horizon. My Navy whites were all muddy. Anyway, to make a long story short I missed the airplane to Hawaii. When I got back to the BOQ I found a magazine with Chuck Lyford's white P-51 on the cover. There was a story about air races scheduled at Reno for September, 1964. I missed the plane to Hawaii to get me around the world so I decided to go to Reno to see what's going on with these piston airplanes."

Lyle dead-headed on an Air Force plane to Reno, rented a car, and checked himself into the BOQ at still active Stead Air Force Base. With directions to Sky Ranch Airport north of Reno, site of the first Reno National Championship Air Races, he drove out to see what was going on.

Growling Merlin engines mixed with the sounds of Wright R-2800 radials, sputtering as they cleared their throats, greeted Lyle when he arrived at Sky Ranch. What he saw was a runway bulldozed out across a dry desert field. Old WW II metal matting covered the sand, sagebrush, and tumbleweed to form the two temporary runways – a 2,000' one for Unlimiteds and a shorter one for the smaller racers. Tanker trucks with sprinklers tried to wet the desert down to keep the dust from blowing. A few bleachers and portable outhouses bordered one side of the field, across the road from the runways. Visitor parking was in the dirt next to the bleachers. There were helicopter landing pads and two or three utility buildings, only one small hangar. Phone lines and high-tension wires ran across the field; highway 33 (Pyramid Highway) ran through the middle of the Unlimited course. Smilin' Jack would have loved this place.

A United Airlines pilot from Van Nuys, California, Clay Lacy and his purple P-51 with the logo of a Conestoga wagon announcing 'Reno or Bust' on the side was attracting a lot of attention from the fans. There were several more P-51s on the field, although a couple had been participants in the cross-country race just completed at the Reno Municipal Airport. Three ex-Navy Grumman F8F Bearcats rounded out the Unlimited entries. Spectators wandered about the pit area watching as mechanics worked on the powerful engines. Afternoon winds whipped sand around the field attacking airplanes, engines and people. The adjacent pit areas held the Biplanes and Midget racing airplanes.

Lyle was more interested in the ex-fighters than in the smaller aircraft. He didn't remember too much about them except their wild-looking paint jobs---"really pretty but awfully small."

Lyle heard one crew chief caution a mechanic to check hose fittings and safety wire the plugs before that plane goes out on the race course. He watched awestruck youngsters staring with fascination at the huge radial or Merlin engines now exposed with their cowlings off. The legendary North American P-51s were close enough to touch. In fact, when he talked to some of the pilots they let him climb up and sit in their cockpits. He got a close look at a couple of Bearcats, the stubby little Navy fighter that came off the assembly line just as WW II was ending. This was the newest fighter in the Grumman 'Cat series built to take off and land on aircraft carriers. Pilots who flew it reported it was fast and agile.

When Lyle returned to the Stead BOQ Friday evening the USAF Thunderbird airplanes were parked at attention in a long row on the ramp waiting for their call to fly Saturday and Sunday. The red, white and blue North American F-100 Super Sabre jets performed a program of loops and rolls, figure 8's, and head-on passes as their smoke trailed white ribbons against the Nevada blue sky.

For the next nine days he stayed the nights at the Stead BOQ and drove the fifteen or so miles to Sky Ranch daily. He didn't think about going around the world. He volunteered to help both Clay Lacy and Walt Ohlrich. Actually, he helped Clay more than Walt. He was fascinated with the purple P-51. Clay was a civilian and more approachable so Lyle got to know him a little better.

"I was a Navy Lieutenant—Walt was a Navy Lt. Commander—so I could be a little more informal with Clay," he exclaimed.

Saturday and Sunday an Autumn Air Show was held at Lake Tahoe Airport featuring Air Force and Navy jets, transports, and helicopters as well as super sophisticated radar-equipped airplanes and a 'fly-over' by fighter-interceptors from the Air Defense Command. Lyle didn't go. He was much more interested in the race planes and pilots at Sky Ranch.

The Unlimiteds flew an 8.019 roughly oval course around hard-to-see pylons. Distance was measured from pylon to pylon. A P-51 flown by Korean war air ace Bob Love set the Unlimited qualifying pace at 395.46 mph with Darryl Greenamyer in a modified F8F Bearcat second at 359.51 mph. Also participating in this historic race were: Clay Lacy in his P-51, Mira Slovak in Bill Stead's Bearcat, Ben Hall in a P-51, Walt Ohlrich in a Bearcat, and E.D. Weiner in a P-51.

Love finished the Gold race first but Slovak was awarded the win based on a complicated point system that had been set up by the race committee using a formula similar to that used for the Unlimited Hydroplane boat racers. Greenamyer had been disqualified for refusing to take off and land at Sky Ranch's narrow runway.

Greenamyer said his cut down canopy makes visibility very difficult while taxiing. "It was a safety concern."

On the final day Washoe Zephers sent dust and sagebrush swirling hundreds of feet in the air. Sand and grit blew into everyone's eyes, ears, mouths, and covered their clothes. Strangers became acquainted as they shared the discomfort and found a common topic of conversation then and in the years to come. "Do you remember that sandstorm?" started conversation at many reunions. There were a lot of jokes about the weather; few pilots or spectators left because of it.

Pilots, crews, and race fans left Sky Ranch in the desert dust each evening and jammed the road back to the neon lights of downtown Reno. Slot machines clattered as coins rattled into the trays below, jackpots were announced with clanging bells and flashing lights, and people laughed or groaned while they watched their money disappear. Lines formed at the Nugget to see Frankie Laine perform in the Circus Room Theater. Harrah's featured Kay Starr and Rich Little in their showroom, while the Vagabonds delighted audiences at the Riverside. The movie theaters showing Sean Connery in 'Dr. No' or the Beatles in 'Hard Day's Night' had record crowds. Bill Stead and his business partners were jubilant.

Lyle joined other pilots and crews gathered around the bar reliving the events of the day. He renewed his acquaintance with Bob Hoover whom he met the year before at a 'Dining In' at Randolph Field. Everybody was in dress uniform at that occasion. One night at the Mapes Hotel in Reno Lyle spotted Hoover partying with some others. He went over and re-introduced himself. Hoover didn't remember Lyle from Randolph but they had a nice talk anyway.

Pilots, crews, spectators, and investors were already talking about a 1965 air race. Stead and his business partners immediately began plans for 'next year'. Lyle was thinking about finding an airplane he could race in 1965.

At the end of the nine days of air racing Lyle continued his thirty-day leave. He bummed a ride on a twin engine Cessna to Salt Lake City where he visited friends. He eventually returned to Randolph Field with some new ideas about his next assignment.

The year 1964 featured several memorable events in addition to the first Reno National Championship Air Races. A British rock music group called the Beatles made their first tour in the United States. Craig Breedlove set a new land speed record of 600 mph in a jet powered car at Bonneville Salt Flats in Utah. Mohammed Ali defeated Sonny Liston in a boxing match. North Viet Nam allegedly attacked United States vessels in the Gulf of Tonkin in August. And Lockheed's beautiful SR-71 Blackbird was shown to the public for the first time.

Those were events Lyle read about in the newspapers or heard about on TV. They really did not affect him personally. His thirty-day leave gave him time to think about the next phase of his life: remain in the Navy; marry a spirited young woman he met in San Antonio; go back to the oil fields; become an air race pilot. He was captivated by the excitement of air racing and wanted to be part of it.

Lyle wanted to fly fast!

04

LYLE'S ROOKIE YEAR

Cables and hoses snaked across the deck, crewmen scurried about, cranes lifted crates and boxes high in the air as Lyle stood in a hatchway watching the activity on the deck of the carrier U.S.S. Kearsage. It was January, 1965, and he had been transferred to Long Beach, California, assigned as a Landing Signal Officer—part of the ship's company—no longer part of the Air Group. He was pleased his request for a West Coast posting has brought him here. He liked his job as Catapult and Arresting Gear Officer although he preferred launching planes over bringing them in for a landing.

"You are up there shooting them off. I felt a bigger part of the action and it was more responsibility. You did not really have much to do with the arresting gear, just make sure that the gear was maintained, seamen taken care, details like that."

As an Air Department Officer he was part of the ship's company where he flew only for proficiency, four hours a month average. He was not happy when he had to watch the planes take off and land every day while he watched from the deck.

Los Angeles was like a different world—congested freeways meandered in all directions crowded with vehicles producing choking smog. Various aircraft manufacturers or aviation-related industries located in and around L.A. had sprawling plants employing hundreds of aeronautical engineers, designers, mechanics and assembly-line workers. Surplus WW II airplanes were inexpensive and available; civilian pilots were buying them to modify for their private use. If he could not find an owner willing to let him race one of his planes Lyle felt he could buy and restore one of the surplus aircraft. There were more than enough qualified people available to help him with such a project.

When he had a day or weekend off Lyle visited small airports to look at warbirds. The most popular of the surplus aircraft was the North American P-51 Mustang; it was the first choice for aspiring race pilots. Lyle was also impressed with the F8F Bearcat.

He said, "The Sea Fury and P-51 will not match the Bearcat in overall performance, in my opinion. It was used by the Navy Blue Angels in the late '40s because of its good performance."

Lyle drove around to the dozens of small airports talking to pilots and mechanics, climbing up on the wing of an airplane and looking at the registration to find out who owned it, then contacting the owner about a deal to race it. One day he saw a P-51 at Chino he liked. Al Redick, a mechanic working there, suggested he call Richard Vartanian, the owner.

Lyle called Vartanian., "I proposed splitting the expenses and any prize monies we won. Finally he and I agreed to enter three unlimited races in 1965: Los Angeles National Air Races at Fox Field in Lancaster, California; Reno National Championship Air Races; Las Vegas International Races in Boulder, Nevada. Vartanian suggested using a P-51 he had just received from South America for the Lancaster race scheduled for May 29 -31, 1965."

Time for repairs ran out before the first race in May so Vartanian and Lyle decided to enter another of Vartanian's P-51s, N#66111.

In August, 1946 Bob Swanson entered #66111 at Cleveland with the name "Full House". It was listed as an F-6K-10…a version of the P-51 used for photo recon. It did not qualify. There was little information on the history of this aircraft between its appearance in the Cleveland races nineteen years earlier and its entry into the current Fox Field race in 1965. For Lyle what mattered was he was a rookie air race pilot in a P-51.

He checked in to Fox Field, a general aviation airport located near Lancaster, California. They were out in the Mojave desert just east of the

Tehachapi mountains and adjacent to Edwards Air Force Base, the huge military airplane testing facility that dominated the area. The blowing desert sand and strong winds swooping down off the Tehachapis reminded Lyle just a little bit of the Reno races the year before. Many of those Reno pilots were entered here at Lancaster: Darryl Greenamyer; Chuck Lyford; E.D. Weiner; Clay Lacy; Mira Slovak; Walt Ohlrich. Grinning happily, Lyle posed in his coveralls with Navy wings over the pocket before the P-51. He obliged fans by climbing into the cockpit for pictures of the rookie race pilot before the race. Then he sat there and surveyed the crowd milling around the field. Lyle finished the Consolation race at 354 mph. Because of gusty winds the Sunday race was postponed for one week; however, Lyle was unable to return to Fox Field for that race because of his airline schedule. The big Reno race was next and he was entered.

The Reno veteran pilots were helpful in briefing the rookie Lyle on the rules so far established for the new sport.

Lacy lived in the Los Angeles area and advised Lyle if he wanted to fly racing airplanes he should get out of the Navy, get an airline pilot's job, and join the Naval Reserve. He could then do all the flying he wanted. Ohlrich, not unapproachable as Lyle imagined, suggested he and Lyle become a team for the Reno race. Other race pilots soon recognized the enthusiasm Lyle had for the sport and encouraged him to "join the group."

Ohlrich knew Rick Blakemore, a WW II Douglas gunner living in Tonopah, Nevada. Blakemore indicated he might be able to raise some sponsorship money for two airplanes if Lyle would like to join Ohlrich as a team. Of course Lyle was eager to do so. He and Ohlrich made their plans and couldn't wait for September.

Tonopah is located in the middle of the state of Nevada. The six-block long main street straddles highway 95, the north-south link between Reno in the north and Las Vegas in the south. In the early 1900s there had been limited gold mining in the area; indeed, mining was once the prime industry here. About ten miles southeast of the highway is the old Tonopah Air Force Base that existed during WW II. Doolittle's Raiders trained there for their B-24 raid on Tokyo.

The sponsorship drive was a bit unorthodox. Ohlrich was supposed to meet Lyle in Tonopah the day before they were due in Reno but he had radio problems when leaving Long Beach. Lyle flew from Chino so they were out of touch. When Lyle got to Tonopah he buzzed it pretty good.

"The last pass I made I came right up the street heading east. I inverted and flew coming up main street upside down. All of a sudden I saw a tall TV tower right in front of me that I hadn't seen before. I shoved forward on the stick, still upside down, missed the TV tower and got a few negative g's, and kind of scared myself. I just went on out to the airport and landed."

Rick met Lyle and took him into town. They worked all the businesses that were open—several were bars—passing the hat.

Then on the way back Lyle tells, "we stopped at a 'cat house'. Bobby's Place—pink stucco, real cheap looking place on the outside. It's kind of hidden by the rocks but you can see it when driving through town. Ole Bobby—she was really a good citizen of the town. It was a pretty nice place inside. Rick and I sat down, had a couple drinks, couple girls came by and talked to us. Bobby gave us more money than anybody else did. I think she gave us about $200 at the time."

The next morning, after Ohlrich got there, Rick wanted them to fly over the school grounds to salute the children. They took off, then Lyle joined up on Ohlrich's wing. They flew by the school grounds, made a couple passes, then headed for Reno. Looking down they could see neat little rows and blocks of children out in the schoolyard waving a sendoff at Lyle in Vartanian's P-51 and Ohlrich in the Bearcat. They used water-based paint to put the names *Tonopah Miss* on the P-51 and *Tonopah Queen* on the Bearcat. They hoped it would not rain and wash the paint off before the end of the week. A few years later pilots had volunteers washing and wiping down their airplane every time they came back from a flight. Oil and dirt on the surface of the wings and fuselage created drag and reduced speed. In the early days, though, the pilots had a lot of fun flying and did not worry about fine-tuning the airplane.

The 1965 Reno National Championship Air Races were held from September 9th to 12th, again at Sky Ranch airport. Northern Nevada weather is never predictable, especially in September. At the beginning of the race week the swirling dust and blowing tumbleweeds that plagued the 1964 races were replaced by swirling black clouds and blowing rainstorms. Lyle was relieved when the storm clouds began clearing by the end of the week. The nine-day event of 1964 was shortened to a five-day event in 1965 (to include qualifying). Highlight of the daily airshow again was the precision flying of the United States Air Force Thunderbirds in their F-100 Super Sabres.

Ten Unlimited qualifiers flew heat races on Friday and Saturday; the championship race was flown on Sunday. Ohlrich and Lyle were among the six planes in the Sunday race. They were pretty excited but did not expect to win. They did plan to fly the fastest they could and have fun doing it. ABC's *Wild World of Sports* filmed the races, trying to make it look close for the home audience. That was difficult because there was not much of a contest among the first four planes. Greenamyer, in *Conquest I*, won easily at 375.10 mph. It turned out Ohlrich and Lyle were pretty closely matched. They were flying in the back of the pack, doing a lot of passing back and forth. When the program was aired several of the other pilots were a little disappointed that Ohlrich and Lyle got so much coverage for their battle for last place.

Lyle had no idea what to expect when flying his first air race at Reno. It was different than the race at Lancaster—more planes, more spectators, larger course, and higher speeds.

Because of his exposure to the Douglas AD Skyraiders in the Navy he felt he was was attracted to the big piston engines. He had a special interest in piston power propeller driven airplanes. He was also fascinated by the performance of the P-51s, Bearcats and Corsairs compared to the slow Skyraider.

He said, "The Skyraider standard squadron cruise was 160-180 knots and at the bottom of a dive from 10,000' I'd see 360 knots full out. In the P-51 I saw 410 knots going straight and level. You always want to fly fast and get better performance out of an airplane."

The Sky Ranch course had its drawbacks—a road cutting through it and power lines crossing it. Lyle didn't care. It had pylons up and he enjoyed flying around them.

"I was a hotter 'n hell pilot and I didn't give a damn. I'd just go like hell and low, you know. It was great fun there in the dirt. I just had a ball. The airplanes were not wired up to destruct power or anything. You'd just kind of go out and jump in and fly off. You were doggone sure you were not going to hurt the engine and were just out there having a great time. Nearly all the guys flying were ex-military who knew what they were doing. It was a good group to fly with. Air racing was in the growing stage where things were not so serious and tight and there weren't so many rules."

The third air racing event in 1965 was the Las Vegas International Air races held at Boulder City airport, September 23-26. The event was marred by a tragic accident during the second heat race. Bob Abrams experienced engine problems, attempted an emergency landing, stalled and crashed fatally. Pilots who entered air races were realists---they knew the risks. They tried to learn what caused the crash and learn from it.

There were nine entries, however Lyle was late arriving and did not qualify to race. He did go out on practice laps. On one pass, when he burned a piston and damaged the cylinder, he declared his first air racing mayday. He was close enough to the field to set up an emergency landing. His experience with carrier landings on a rocking deck was trickier by far than this little problem. The emergency landing was uneventful; however the return flight to Chino was a little scary. His mechanic, "Supe" (Supervisor) Hoisington, just pulled the wires off a burned cylinder and told Lyle to fly it back to Chino on the remaining eleven cylinders. Lyle was speechless. He thought Hoisington was kidding but, no, "Supe" told Lyle he would go with him. When the races were over Hoisington and Lyle climbed into the P-51 and added power but it was so rough Lyle aborted the take-off.

Hoisington told him, "Just leave the power up there", so they taxied back and started another take-off roll.

Hoisington encouraged Lyle to keep the throttle up and they finally lifted off and flew back to Chino with one cylinder totally dead. Lyle got used to the shaking and rattling and they made it OK.

All in all, Lyle's rookie year as an air race pilot had been memorable.

05

CHANGING A CAREER

On January 31, 1966, Lyle officially ended his career with the Navy. The next day he was out of the Navy and at the TWA training center in downtown Kansas City, Kansas, learning to be an airline pilot. He started at the bottom of the seniority roster as a flight engineer on Boeing 727s as 'reserve pilot on standby.' The airline called him in to fly as needed.

Mike Carroll was rebuilding a Sea Fury in Long Beach and Lyle wanted to fly in the Reno races in September. He flew out to Long Beach and talked Carroll into letting him fly it (the Sea Fury) that year.

Bill Stead, the driving force behind the two-year old Reno races, survived several years during WW II in Britain's Royal Air Force as well as many years of racing hydroplane boats; he did not survive air racing. Although he owned an F8f-2 Bearcat he did not race it. He chose to begin racing in the small, demanding Midget class. In April, 1966, he was in Florida practicing in his recently purchased Sorenson midget racer, *Deerfly*, when a bolt apparently came off the elevator control. He lost control of the airplane and crashed fatally into Tampa Bay.

There was a lot of speculation about the future of the Reno races after Stead's death. It was a tribute to his planning and organization that the Reno Air Race Association could continue with the plans already in progress for the 1966 race. Stead had proved spectators would come to a remote section of Nevada if he brought fast airplanes and daring pilots together for them to watch. The Air Race Association continued to advertise days filled with speedy planes and nights filled with the glitz, glitter, and glamour of the Reno casinos.

When they arrived for the 1966 air races the pilots were pleased to see the venue for the races move to Stead Field, the former Army Air Force flight training field where Lyle had stayed in 1964. The facility was operated by the General Services Administration during the transition period before being annexed by the city of Reno. In later years the Washoe County Airport Authority took over its operation. The field was named in honor of Lieutenant Croston Stead, Bill Stead's brother, who had been a member of the Nevada Air National Guard when he was killed in a crash there in 1949.

The move to Stead meant better conditions for the planes and pilots; it also meant improved facilities for the spectators. With its longer, paved runways, no power lines or country roads on the course and acres of parking the field was ideally suited for the plans the Reno Air Race Association had to expand and promote air racing.

When Lyle arrived at Stead in Mike Carroll's Sea Fury he was one of eleven Unlimited entries. Carroll had modified the Sea Fury by cutting the canopy down, clipping the wing tips and trying to install a water injection system. The plane looked like a racer with its jazzy paint job but there were problems flying it--- it would bleed speed badly in the turns. He had no crew standing by. Volunteers eagerly helped the pilots clean oil off the aircraft and give the pilot a lift up to the cockpit. There were other control problems, however Lyle was able to coax it into a second place finish in the Saturday consolation race, coming in at 353.89 mph

Carroll was killed the next year after he flew out of Seal Beach Weapons Depot, southeast of Long Beach, in a P-39. Greenamyer and Lyle both volunteered to test fly the P-39 but Carroll had declined. He had about 350 hours or so and thought he could test it himself. He got off with E.D. Weiner chasing him. He lost control and tried to bail out right after take-off over Seal Beach; he hit the tail jumping out of the airplane and the chute never opened. Lyle and the other race pilots mourned the loss of their friend and fellow air racer. They all realized this was fun...and it was serious business.

After qualifying first at 409.972 mph it was no surprise when Greenamyer won the gold race at Reno on Sunday. The winning speed was a slow 396.22 mph.

At the end of three years of racing at Reno there were pilots, mechanics, engineers, and designers in all classes eager to modify a piston engine airplane to make it the fastest in its class. Lyle was among them; he had a severe case of air racing fever.

Between World War I and World War II many United States Army Air service pilots flew military aircraft in air races because the Army felt it was a good place to test the newest designs.

As General Hap Arnold sat in the grandstands at an early air race watching a small plane powered by a 400 hp engine keeping up with Roscoe Turner, in a Wedell-Turner airplane powered by an 825 hp Pratt & Whitney Hornet radial engine, the General is quoted as saying "I think there is still a lot we need to know about airplanes and engines."

Designers watched and learned. Frontal resistance problems led to streamlined cowlings. Overheated engines led to water-cooled engines. High wings versus low wings versus mid wings produced varying flight characteristics and radically different wing designs. Pilots experimented with weight reduction measures to increase speed. The list went on and on.

When military expenditures for development of racing aircraft stopped civilian designed and tested aircraft such as the Laird Solution, Seversky SEV, and the Gee Bees, to name a few, appeared in their place. Pilots whose names we still revere—"Speed" Holman, Jimmy Doolittle, Jimmy Wedell, Roscoe Turner—won the Thompson Trophy, successor to the Pulitzer Trophy. Almost all WW II airplanes actually flown in combat were on the drawing board or in limited production when the conflict started in 1939.

Rolls Royce was pressured by Britain's Air Ministry to develop an engine for the 1929 Schneider Trophy race. The specter of negative publicity if the engine failed made Henry Royce apprehensive about getting involved in an air racing project; however, he accepted the challenge. Facing an almost impossible deadline of one year to produce the new racing engine, Rolls Royce decided to modify an existing engine—the Rolls Royce Buzzard. The new Rolls Royce 'R' engine featured a supercharger with a two-sided impeller with dual intakes which developed manifold pressure of 55 inches Hg (high gain), unheard of at the time. R. J. Mitchell designed the fuselage of the Supermarine S6 to accommodate the supercharger housing of the new 'R' engine. The Supermarine S6 won the 1929 Schneider Trophy race at 328 mph and then went on to establish a new world air-speed record of 357.7 mph.

The goal of all racers was speed so designers concentrated their efforts on more horsepower and better streamlining; however, flying the fastest airplane did not mean flying the most reliable or best handling airplane. Howard Hughes proved that in his H-1 Special by supervising every detail of its construction. It was reliable and aerodynamically clean but not the fastest around the pylons. Hughes never raced it but did set the transcontinental speed record in 1937 of 7 hours 28 minutes, something none of the sprint racers could do.

The air racing community directly or indirectly contributed other innovations that were to benefit the Allied air fleets in the following decade. The experience Rolls Royce gained during the 'R' racing engine project—designing, developing, testing, and meeting deadlines—served the company well as WW II engulfed Europe. Their name on their products signified quality to their customers. Their two-sided impeller design led to the two-sided centrifugal impeller design in the early Whittle and Rolls Royce gas turbine engines. Detonation-resistant fuel developed by Rodwill Banks consisting of 78% benzole and 22% Romanian petrol plus 2 cm per gallon tetraethyl lead was used to help the Supermarine S6 win the 1929 Schneider race. A similar formula was later used during WW II in Allied aircraft engines to improve their efficiency. The use of ram air induction for the blower intake, patented in 1927 by Rolls Royce was in common use during the conflict giving as much as a 10% increase in horsepower to most aircraft engines. Civilian designers race tested innovations such as retractable landing gear, landing flaps, ventilated cockpits, air-cooled engines, and controllable pitch propellers which were modified, used and improved upon on wartime aircraft of all nations.

When Lyle arrived in California many designers who had worked on those war-time projects were now employed by aircraft manufacturers in the Los Angeles area. Engineers with experience producing engines for the wartime fleet were available to give advice when Lyle began his restoration of his Bearcat. Volunteer designers, engineers and mechanics continued to pursue increasing the speed of WW II airplanes using air racers as their test vehicles.

Lyle listened and learned as pilots, engineers, and crews debated the merits of each innovation on each air racer. He knew he could not borrow an airplane to modify. During a conversation with Alan Paulsen, head of Gulfstream Corporation, they discussed putting a Wright R-3350 engine in a Bearcat. Paulsen speculated the combination would produce a great race plane.

"Well Al," Lyle replied, "I flew 3350s in Skyraiders in the Navy and they did not have a good reputation for reliability. That conversation broadened my scope because at that time I was looking for a wrecked P-51 and was going to put a Griffon engine on it. In 1965 there was a P-51 up in Tonopah that sold for $5,000. It was not in the best shape but it was a fairly decent airplane. Up until racing started you could find a decent, flyable P-51 for around $5,000 to $6,000. After that, by 1969, a pretty good Bearcat cost about $20,000."

As Lyle studied the history of changes ---and their results---to various airplanes, he knew he could modify a WW II fighter to go faster. He was determined to find one he could afford.

While continuing his search for an aircraft he could turn into an air racer Lyle moved up in the TWA ranks to flight engineer on Boeing 707s, still on reserve. He welcomed his transfer back to Los Angeles in 1967 where he began flying out of Los Angeles International Airport (LAX).

A large, strong family surrounded Lyle through his school years. It was replaced by his Navy "family" for almost a decade. While in San Antonio he was introduced to a petite, attractive widow, Joyce Slack. The handsome Naval officer and lively young widow dated, sometimes bringing Joyce's four-year-old son with them to see the Navy airplanes up close on the field. Joyce shared Lyle's love for airplanes and little John was fascinated by the big Navy fighters In 1966 Joyce and John moved to Long Beach to be near Lyle. In 1967 Lyle and Joyce married as he continued his TWA career, joined the Naval Reserve, and pursued his dream of building an air racer.

He had a new family, a new job, and no airplane. Lyle missed flying in the 1967 and 1968 Reno races. He attended both years, renewed acquaintances, continued asking for leads on wrecks he could restore and modify and watched longingly as Greenamyer cruised to win the Gold Unlimited races in his Bearcat, *Conquest I.*

06

Birth of the Rare Bear

In 1965 Walt Ohlrich was serving as liaison between the Navy and McDonnell Douglas. When he showed Lyle a picture of a wrecked Bearcat laying in a field near the Valparaiso, Indiana airport. Lyle said it was too far gone. Three years later he heard about a Hellcat owned by Mike Coutches. He flew up to the Hayward, California airport, looked over the airplane and decided it was too corroded. He and Coutches talked about his search for a wreck he could rebuild as a racer. Coutches mentioned a Bearcat he had in Indiana. It was the same wrecked plane Ohlrich had shown Lyle earlier.

Lyle inspects wreckage, 1968.
Shelton Collection

In early 1968, while on a layover at Chicago's O'Hare airport, Lyle drove to Valparaiso to look at Coutches' wrecked airplane. This wasn't the worst he had seen, nor was it the best. Two main sections lay in the weeds behind a small building. Two wings—minus tips—with the cockpit section between them rested on the ground. The fuselage, aft of the cockpit section, was in one piece and reasonably intact. Odd pieces and parts were strewn around. When the wing/cockpit section was raised it exposed a partial left landing gear. There was no sign of the right gear. The list of missing parts was longer than the inventory of what was there. As he stood in the weeds amongst the scattered aircraft parts he decided to buy it if the price was right. Coutches asked $2,500, plus California sales tax. It seemed a fair price so Lyle bought it.

Lyle thought this particular airplane was originally sold out of North Island, San Diego, California. Those Bearcats were sold in batches of twenty-five in 1959 or 1960. One guy got them all for $800 each. He then sold them off individually. This one was bought by Frank Tallman and Paul Mantz at Riverside. Then it was re-sold to someone in Miami, Florida.

Years later Lyle received a book titled *I NEVER FLEW ALONE* by Donald E. Dresselhaus describing the flight of the Bearcat from Miami to Valdosta, Georgia. A Lake Geneva, Wisconsin businessman had purchased the aircraft for $6,000; he then hired Dresselhaus to fly the plane from Miami to Wisconsin. During a refueling stop in Valdosta a curious spectator pulled the wrong lever; the canopy was damaged when it fell to the ground. Dresselhaus had to leave the aircraft there for repair. In August, 1962, after repairs, a second pilot was hired to fly the aircraft from Valdosta to Porter County Airport near Valparaiso, Indiana. Dresselhaus was on hand at the airport to take over and fly the remaining distance to Lake Geneva. He watched as the Bearcat lined up the runway then went out of control. After a hard landing and hydraulic failure, the plane cartwheeled down and off the runway landing upside down in the dirt with the pilot still strapped in his seat in the cockpit. Dresselhaus, some bystanders, and the local fire department were able to dig the slightly injured pilot out; however, the plane was severely damaged. The intended owner abandoned it, giving up his plans to make it into an aerobatic performer. Eventually the plane was dragged to the back of someone's hangar where it lay in a weed patch for the next six years.

When Lyle purchased it the plane had been stripped of gear fairings, engine, engine mount, all instruments, cockpit controls , all hydraulic system actuators, valves, etc.

In April, 1968, Lyle went to Valparaiso and concentrated on getting the wrecked Bearcat from Indiana to California Lyle donned his coveralls and recruited some local help. They drilled more than 500 rivets fastening the fuselage and wing sections, separated them from the tail cone section, then knocked the airplane apart. Most of the big pieces fit onto a rented flat bed truck he drove to O'Hare airport. The rest he shipped to California on one of the Flying Tigers swing-tailed CL-44s.

"Somehow, being an airline employee, I got a discount and was able to stuff about half the pieces on that cargo plane. That is how I got some of it back to Compton."

The wings and center section are one big unit. Lyle took that section about twenty miles northwest of O'Hare airport to Earl Rhinert's place, the dealer who had the airplane before he sold it to Mike Coutches. Rhinert had some storage space there with a bunch of old warbirds and a makeshift museum.

It was November, 1968 before Lyle had enough money to go back to Chicago. He bought a green Chevrolet half-ton pickup truck and a trailer to tow the wing/fuselage section to California. All went well until he got into New Mexico. In a previous flight into the small Las Vegas, New Mexico airport Lyle had seen a disassembled Grumman *Wildcat* next to a hangar at the field.

"The same hangar we used in 1989 during the 3-km speed run.," he said.

The Wildcat was not there so Lyle continued his trip in a snowstorm. Between Las Vegas and Santa Fe, as he was rounding the south end of the Sacramento Mountains, he temporarily lost control of the truck and trailer. The snowy, slippery unplowed road wound through the high desert and that day there were few other vehicles around to watch as he struggled to keep from going over the edge and down the cliff. It was a harrowing experience as the trailer wobbled towards the icy edge of the road. When the trailer and truck straightened out he continued slowly along the winding highway, determined the wreckage he was towing was going to become an air racer.

Two days later he pulled into Chino where he left the trailer in a tie-down spot until he could rent a T-hangar closer to his home in Long Beach. In late January, 1969, he moved the wrecked pieces of the F8F-2 Grumman Bearcat, registry number N1031B, into a hangar at Compton, California.

Bill Hickle, a curly-haired young Structures Engineer, was working the swing shift at Northrop doing structural repair design in 1969. The North Dakota State University graduate was trained on reverse engineering—looking at something and determining what its strength was and what it probably did by examining it and the surrounding structure. After breakfast in the morning he went to Compton Airport to work on a Curtiss-Robin airplane he had hangared there, then on to work at Northrop in the afternoon. As he drove in to the field one day he observed several workers offloading a flat bed trailer. The load intrigued him....pieces and parts of an old Navy fighter plane. Hickle introduced himself and asked a lot of questions about their project. The guys were using a forklift trying to put the fuselage of the old Bearcat hulk onto a metal framework in the hangar. The tall, lanky crew chief, Cliff Putman, explained the problem they were having. Lyle joined the group and asked Hickle if there was anyone around who could weld. Hickle had his welder in his hangar close by so he volunteered.

They wanted to erect a framework made of flat metal upright and horizontal bars, crossed and braced in the hangar, then mount the wing/cockpit section on the framework. Some alterations were needed to make it fit together. Once the welding was done they used a forklift to place the fuselage center section onto the framework. It was supported in a horizontal position about six or seven feet off the floor. Between the two wing sections was the center section from the cockpit to the firewall. Parts of the landing gear assembly dangled beneath the wings; wires stuck out in all directions.

Hickle designed an engine mount and did some other structural engineering for Lyle. Design repairs were needed because the airplane was really beat up. The rear wing spar was badly damaged and there was other major structural damage. The engineering advice Hickle was able

Ready to Begin, Compton, 1969.
Pete Behenna

to share with the crew was instrumental in getting the restoration of the Bearcat started,

Lyle said, "Bill Hickle has been a key part of the *Rare Bear Air Racing Team* since that first day when he walked up and introduced himself."

There were some guidelines for Lyle to follow rebuilding the Bearcat.

THE OFFICIAL PROFESSIONAL RACE PILOTS ASSOCIATION FOR UNLIMITED CLASS AIRPLANES READ:

Item 2:   <u>ENGINE AND PROPELLER</u>

1. Aircraft must be propeller driven and powered by a reciprocating engine or engines.

2. There are no restrictions on engine modification.

3. No aerodynamic turbine or rocket thrust devices may be used.

Item 3:   <u>AIRFRAME</u>

1. There are no restrictions on airframe modifications.

Item 4:   MAXIMUM WEIGHT

1. Aircraft must not have a gross weight over 21,000 pounds.   Maximum gross weight is 21,000 pounds.

Item 5:   FUEL AND FUEL TANKS

1. Any type of fuel or additives may be used.

2. Aircraft must have fuel tankage to enable it to operate at race power plus twenty minutes at orbiting power. Heat races shall never exceed ten laps of one hundred miles.

3. No aerodynamic turbine or rocket thrust devices may be used.

The search for parts took Lyle all over the United States. When Bob Kucera crashed fatally in his photogrammetry equipped Bearcat Lyle bought quite a few of the salvaged parts from Mrs. Kucera. Ernie Saviano, an American Airlines pilot, crashed a Bearcat at the airport in Madison Wisconsin, when he lost the engine on approach, then went upside down in the swamp at the north end of the airport. Lyle went to Madison and salvaged flaps, elevators, rudder, and part of the tail. He and Gunther Balz met there while they both waded waist deep in the swamp. Balz was also salvaging pieces for his Bearcat. When the Confederate Air Force's Lloyd Nolan had to land a Bearcat on one wheel, putting the plane out of commission for a while, Lyle borrowed their windscreen and canopy for about a year. Then he borrowed a wing tip and aileron from Bill Fornof in Houma, Louisiana.

To get those parts back to Compton Lyle waited until he had two weeks active duty in the Los Alamitos A-4 Squadron down in Roosevelt Roads, Puerto Rico. On his return he landed at New Orleans NAS, rented a car, drove down to Houma and made a deal with Fornof for the wing tip and aileron. The squadron support plane, a C-118 (also known as a DC-4 or R5D) had landed at New Orleans so Lyle was able to truck the parts up and have them loaded for the trip back to Los Alamitos.

He bought the nose bowl and cowling in Connecticut from a surplus airplane parts dealer.

Pete Behenna, another of the original crew, was working at American Airlines. They were on strike when Lyle called the union hall to ask if someone would like to work. Behenna, an amateur photographer, volunteered. Harry Smith, a sheet metal worker, was cutting and welding metal but needed help holding the pieces and doing the riveting. The rugged-looking, dark-haired, hard-working Behenna helped Smith; then took on some of the myriad jobs that were needed. He also took time to record the rebuilding of the airplane. His first picture was the wing/fuselage/dangling gear as it sat on the framework in the hangar. The work progressed; Behenna recorded scenes in the busy hangar with Putman, Hickle, Lyle, and Smith as an aircraft grew out of the jumble of parts on the hangar floor.

Wings were coming off in flight on some of the Navy Bearcats in the late 1940s and early 1950s. Navy engineers remedied this by putting a strap under the bottom side of the wing spar external to the airplane. It was an ugly strip and it was still on the salvaged airplane. Lyle and Hickle decided they would not be pushing the plane like the Navy did on carriers so they chopped the strip off the bottom. That left the wing with its original contour and smoothness. They called it 'eyeball engineering.'

The Wright R-3350 engine was Lyle's choice to replace the Pratt & Whitney R-2800, originally used on Grumman Bearcats. He had done his homework on the size and weight of the engine. Richard Tracy, a brilliant aeronautical engineer, was living in Huntington Beach and available for consultations regarding the design modifications Lyle wanted to make. Lyle questioned the propeller thrust line. Hickle and Tracy knew the Bearcat's engine originally was pointed down at six degrees. That six degree down thrust gave the airplane better longitudinal stability, or pitch, in its design ranges for general handling, general dog-fighting and combat purposes.

Hickle thought, "If we are going to go fast we're going to point the engine straight ahead. Richard allowed as we shouldn't do that so we compromised and now the engine is pointed down three degrees. That's why when we had the standard Bearcat cowling on it you could see a little wedge on the cowling around the engine because we had changed the alignment."

Now that the mechanics knew what engine they would use, and the thrust angle was modified, Hickle had to design a new engine mount. The engine had to go as close to the firewall by the leading edge of the wing as possible. They went from there, reverse engineered and calculated some G-loads the engine would carry ---close to 25g's---designed the engine mount to support the Wright R-3350-26 18 cylinder two-row radial air-cooled engine and the Hamilton Standard DC-7 propeller, with the loads on it, and position it properly. To do this, they clamped the engine mount ring, which attaches to the engine, on a framework--- and on the other end of that framework they installed the fittings that go on the fuselage and cut the tubes between them. For the first few years the rest of the airplane was basically stock—except where the cowling was slightly displaced.

Lyle went to George Byard of Aircraft Cylinder and Turbine in Sun Valley, California to find a Wright R-3350 engine. Byard thought they had one out in the back yard waiting to be salvaged for parts and recovery of precious metals it contains, The engine was open, unplugged, no stacks, and rain water had gotten into the cylinders. Lyle said he wanted it and George ended up donating it to him.

Crew Chief George Putman cleaned out the bird's nests, sticks, cobwebs and other debris and managed to rebuild the engine. He got help from the skilled mechanics at Aircraft Cylinder.

There were a lot of discussions about the reliability of the Wright 3350. "If you get the right components it is a well-designed engine," said Lyle.

"Wright really had well engineered piston engines before the end of that era. The B-29s with those early 3350s , they were lucky to get 300 hours engine time out of them. The later engines, though, were really good engines."

Lyle's decision to mate the Bearcat wreck to a surplus Wright R-3350 engine was the first major step in the evolution of the *Rare Bear*.

There was a cheering section of about twenty-five people standing around the first time they tried to start the engine. Lyle cranked it thirty to forty times before it fired up and then the spectators made about as much noise as the engine did. Shouts, hurrahs, and foot-stamping

Working on Engine No. 1
Pete Behenna

erupted as the relieved crew saw success in the smoke of that old, noisy engine. It was a big step towards getting the Bearcat in the air.

Finally, in August, Behenna took a picture of a recognizable aircraft parked on the ramp in front of the hangar. Lyle's young stepson, John Slack, stood on the wing as he peered into the empty cockpit. The weary crew didn't have much time for celebrating…it was almost time for FAA certification and flight testing.

In another hangar at Compton John Marlin was restoring and modifying a P-51, later raced as *Daydreamer*. He recalls that some days there were as many as ten guys working on the Bearcat project.

"Tony Bernard did sheet metal work; Bill Kientz was busy with electrical work; Harry Smith and Pete Behenna did a lot of fabricating on the cowling. Lyle was so nice to everyone. He brought cokes and Pepsis and sent someone out on hog dog runs. Joyce and their friends, Angela and Joe Barbero, brought sandwiches. The guys worked diligently, sometimes eight to ten hours a day, depending who was available. It was a concentrated effort by everybody but we had a lot of fun. It wasn't a frustrating project at all. They got the gears cleaned up, then they got the engine mount made, and Lyle was worrying about where he was going to get an engine. Then he got that squared away. Then he had prop problems and had to use the DC-7 prop with a long, pointed spinner. Actually, that worked quite well."

Lyle was looking for a DC-7 or AD Skyraider propeller when he stumbled across several DC-7 props somewhere in the San Fernando valley. DC-7 props were not in demand then. He was able to buy a Hamilton Standard prop with solid aluminum blades, and a spinner, for about $150. It had a big, heavy nose dome with all the reversing mechanism that they did not really need, but it was a real slick aerodynamic prop. It did add extra weight and was replaced in the third year with a lighter weight AD prop.

At the end of summer in 1969 they saw a real airplane sitting in the hangar. Lyle had vivid memories of the wreck towed onto the field in January. The airplane in the hangar represented a small miracle. Of course, he was anxious to fly it!

A weight and balance check indicated that the CG (center of gravity) needed adjusting. They corrected the problem by adding about 200 pounds of lead in the form of bars and lead beads into the tail section. When it was time to do the first test flights Lyle did not want to risk making the initial take-off from Compton's short 3,400' runway. It meant they must tow the airplane to a larger airport.

One hot summer night Behenna and the crew towed the Bearcat on its wheels, wings folded, from Compton Airport to Long Beach Airport. They tried to get the airport manager there to approve the plane for take off but he would not do it. A few months earlier Mike Carroll had taken off from Long Beach in a P-39 he had recently restored. He lost control and tried to bail out but crashed fatally into the Seal Beach Weapons Depot. The Long Beach airport manager felt there was too much risk to approve another experimental airplane make its first flight in that congested area.

A few nights later the crew made another middle of the night zigzag journey towing the Bearcat through city streets, this time from the Long Beach airport, for about twenty miles to the Orange County Airport. In 1969 the Orange County Airport was in the middle of fields of crops and groves of fruit trees. They were not hindered by overhead electrical and phone wires. About 3:00 a.m. the procession passed a little neighborhood bar that was just closing. Several less than sober patrons were wondering if they were really seeing an airplane driving by on the street. There was a lot of laughter and jokes from both the bar patrons and the Bearcat crew members. By the time the crew finished dragging the airplane over the rough pavement the solid rubber tail wheel was worn out and had to be replaced.

After he explained his intended departure path would avoid any congested areas if he lost an engine and he would not plow into houses or industry, the Orange County airport manager gave permission to Lyle to take off. The Federal Aviation Administration inspector then came out to certify the Bearcat as airworthy.

Finally, on September 13, 1969, six days before the start of the Reno races, Lyle did a couple high speed taxi runs. The numbers looked OK. Next he lifted the airplane into the air and set it back down. Everything was still OK. The crew was elated but no one felt as exhilarated as Lyle. There was a huge grin on his face as he taxied back to the ramp, refueled, and announced he would fly to the Chino airport. Observing and taking pictures of this first flight were several members of the American Aviation Historical Society.

None of Lyle's Navy flying experiences compared to this first flight in his own air racer! He could not resist flying the Bearcat around the Chino area. It was an incredible feeling after all the obstacles he and the crew had overcome to actually have the Bearcat in the air. Like the make-believe airplane he rode at the Dallas Fairground many years before, he didn't want to come down.

Ready to Race at Reno, 1969.
Pete Behenna

Reluctantly, he landed and left the plane with "Supe" Hoisington and the guys at Aerosport until he could return and take off for Reno. In the meantime the crew commuted from Compton to work on the engine and paint the plane with yellow zinc chromate primer. They wanted to put a finish coat on it but everyone had been working so hard they did not have enough energy to put on the next coat of paint.

When asked how he named his plane, Lyle answered, "I liked flying the big Skyraider AD (Able Dog) in the Navy so I called my Bearcat 'Able Cat'."

John Marlin painted a big race number 70 in black numbers on it and it was ready to go racing.

07

RENO!

Prior to flying to Reno in September, 1969, there had been time for only two test flights around Chino. When time ran out the crew packed their tools and drove to Reno. After their arrival they were continually testing and checking out the various squawks and mechanical problems. There were a lot, which was to be expected. During the ferry flight from Chino to Reno Lyle found several problems with the hydraulics and other systems and components. They were running the engine at 2,900 rpms, wide open throttle, but only getting about 3,000hp. In spite of that, Lyle was able to qualify sixth at 357.65 mph.

According to the National Air-racing Group's Time-to-Speed handout, this is how qualifying is conducted:

"Qualifying runs require 2 laps. A pilot may abort the run at any time by pulling up off the course, but must then repeat the entire sequence. Flags: green, white, checkered. For radio-equipped raceplanes, the pilot alerts Reno Air Race Association's timers via aircraft radio, calling in before Pylon 4. Timing starts as the raceplane crosses Home Pylon, and both laps are timed. The faster time of the 2 laps is the qualifying time. General: A pylon cut on a timing lap negates that lap; the pilot may try again only after all others have qualified. If no time remains, 4 seconds per cut is added to the time lap for the official time."

Darryl Greenamyer was small in stature but a formidable competitor in *Conquest 1* He lived in nearby Lancaster; he had met and adjusted to the quirky winds and the swirling sandstorms that swept into Mojave from the Tehachapi Mountains. He was the strongest contender entered and easily won the Gold race on Sunday at 412.631 mph for his fourth Reno air race win. Lyle placed fifth at 356.366 mph.

When asked, what is the basic difference between his aircraft and *Conquest 1*, Lyle explained, "First , a bigger engine. They have a Pratt & Whitney R-2800 and we're running a Wright R-3350 and we're doing our cooling differently. They went to a boil off oil cooling system which is a little less drag so we're running a little more drag on the oil cooling. That's the biggest thing. We're heavier by about 500 pounds. And Greenamyer took a lot of weight out by taking all his hydraulic gear out. He has an air bottle to blow the gear up and he drops the gear manually. All we operate on our hydraulic system are the two main gear and the tail wheel. We figure that gives a reliability factor. Also we run a different propeller. Greenamyer has clipped the wings and uses a cut down canopy. *Able Cat* has a fairly stock Bearcat configuration."

The Bearcat crew and Lyle felt pretty good about their first year of racing. They were rookies. They watched crews with matching, colorful uniforms strutting across the ramps to their pits. Some of the race planes had eye-catching paint jobs that attracted dozens of photographers. Lyle was not disappointed in his Bearcat. Those to whom he showed pictures of the wreck next to a hangar in Indiana were impressed with *Able Cat* sitting on the ramp in Reno in 1969. The crew was proud of their entry. Eye-catching paint schemes on the airplane made good pictures but didn't improve the speed in the air. The crew concentrated on the big powerful engine that would get the aircraft around the pylons faster than the rest of the pack. They felt the glory was just ahead of them.... after they did some more tweaking and tuning. They had gained a lot of experience and confidence without attracting a lot of attention.

Lyle spent about $20,000 of his own money to buy the parts they needed. The aircraft they finally certified for air racing was so highly modified many of its parts were custom made. Mechanics faced a challenge when they worked on it.

Able Cat's crew felt the thrill of being in the pits as part of the air race; they were impressed as they watched the United States Air Force

Thunderbirds perform in their Phantom jets. It was apparent to all that the race pilots each had a strategy to fly the course...some staying high and out of traffic, others close in and tight around the pylons. Lyle enjoyed the racing. He watched the different planes fly and mentally noted what he liked and what, as a former instructor, he criticized. As owner of the airplane he was interested in equipment that might be useful on the Bearcat.

The crew made do with two rooms at the Riverside Hotel, some sleeping on rollaway beds or sleeping bags. The expenses for the round-trip between Chino and Reno that year cost Lyle about $3,000. By 1995 the size of the crew increased, fuel prices increased, engines and repair part prices sky-rocketed, bringing Lyle's costs for air race week to approximately $30,000. (Insurance was not included in this figure as RARA had a blanket liability policy at that time.)

In July, 1969, millions of people watched their TV sets as a project costing millions of NASA/tax-payer dollars and millions of man-hours culminated with Neil Armstrong making 'one giant step for mankind' onto the surface of the moon. In September that same year a few thousand spectators watched as Lyle Shelton's hybrid air racer costing thousands of Lyle's dollars and hundreds of volunteer man-hours flew its memorable first race around the pylons at Stead Field near Reno, Nevada.

Lyle knew he and the crew were on the right path with modifications to the Bearcat . After the 1969 Reno races they went back to southern California to continue working on the engine. They put in a new water injection cooling system and rebuilt the engine and hydraulic system. Drag reducing modifications were made to the fuselage. They even had time to paint *Able Cat* a bright yellow with blue trim.

At the 1970 Reno races the engine modifications and fuselage streamlining work done during the year paid off with improved speeds. Lyle qualified fifth in a field of fourteen with a speed of 373.460 mph—17.1 mph faster than 1969. He went on to win his first heat race at 369.268 mph using regular 115/145 PN high octane gasoline. Both the military and commercial airliners used it in the R-3350 and R-4360 engines.

On Sunday the temperatures dropped, scattered clouds moved in, and the winds picked up. The Unlimited pilots knew this Gold race would be a rough ride. The Bearcat's new race number was #77 but double sevens did not bring luck that day. On the first lap the engine detonated, damaging some cylinders, and forced Lyle to mayday. The engine was one of the old surplus 3350s on which there had been no history. When it blew nobody was sure what happened. The crew thought they had fixed a problem with the water injection system. Or maybe it was the racing fuel Lyle was using. He had consulted with experienced engine mechanics about fuel mixtures.

Able Cat and Crew, 1970.
Shelton Collection

"We were lead to believe that we could load a whole bunch of nitro methane into the tank," Lyle admits. "We had been advised by a real nice old guy—a Champion Spark Plug representative—how much of that stuff we could use. We loaded about five to ten times too much methane right into the tank and that stuff was going right into the cylinders and just exploding as soon as I added power. We were in the pole position for that race, I think, and Clay Lacy was second or third, but we had loaded so much of that nitro methane that just as soon as I put the throttle forward and turned the water on, it started blowing the engine. I made it about half way around, then started to pull up and landed on north-south runway 18. That is the closed runway that goes past the Air National Guard hangar in the northwest area of the field."

The other racers pulled up to give Lyle room to maneuver for his emergency landing. Bob Hoover was circling overhead calling out to Lyle how much runway he had left before he would have to ground loop. When Hoover said, "Now!" Lyle hit the rudder hard, spun around, and went over a piece of concrete laying to one side. It was not any kind of fixture, just junk hiding out in the weeds. The tail wheel slammed into the concrete which hit the fuselage right above the wheel. It tore the tail wheel right off the airplane. The retrieval crew used a tall crane to pick up the airplane, then wrapped a strap around it under its tail and put the tail on a dolly. The plane was towed to a corner of the field until repairs could be made and Lyle could fly it back to Compton.

Wearing a bright purple flight suit Clay Lacy won the race in his matching purple P-51, *Miss Van Nuys*, at a speed of 387.342 mph. Greenamyer's winning streak ended at five when his right landing gear failed to fully retract. He flew the race with the partially retracted gear hanging like a bent elbow under *Conquest 1*.

After the race Lyle and George Williamson trucked the Bearcat engine back to Compton. The engine was junk so they got a new one from Aircraft Cylinder. They found an R-3350 built after WW II by Wright Aeronautical Corporation that had been used in an airliner. The paper work on the engine didn't identify which airliner had previously used the engine. These airliner engines were stronger, more durable and much better suited to be used and modified for air racing. Steel forged crankcases replaced the original aluminum forged crankcases. New, tougher metals were used for many parts such as master rods and cylinders. The crew worked hard that winter to modify and test the new engine before they would be ready to enter the 1971 Reno races.

Since the Bearcat was recuperating after Reno Lyle could not enter it in the California 1,000 Air Race held November 15, 1970 at the Mojave Airport, California. He did, however, pair with Bob Metcalf to fly relief in a Hawker Sea Fury. They finished fourth, completing sixty-one laps, after making one pit stop. The race was won by Sherm Cooper flying non-stop in his spectacular Sea Fury. His time was two hours, fifty-two minutes, thirty-eight seconds. The race attracted nationwide attention because of one extraordinary entry—Clay Lacy flying a DC-7B! With Alan Paulsen flying co-pilot the lumbering giant flew non-stop for sixty laps to finish in sixth place.

08

First Victory

After the 1970 Reno races the Bearcat remained at Stead Field while back in the Compton hangar Mel Gregoire, Bill Coulter and George Williamson built the first of many hybrid R-3350 engines. Mel was working at Aircraft Cylinder when his boss donated the R-3350 to Lyle. A WW II Army Engineer veteran, Mel had also worked for Grand Central Company, the West Coast representative for the Wright Engine Company. He was experienced working on the Wright R-3350 engines destined for use on DC-7s and Lockheed Constellations. Adapting the R-3350 to the Bearcat gave Mel the opportunity to modify some elements he felt would improve its performance. One of his first efforts was to redesign the supercharger.

The early Wright 3350 engines had a standard propeller shaft reduction gear ratio (16:7) which resulted in rather high prop blade tip speeds on the big DC-7 prop that was installed on the Bearcat. Lyle consulted with Charlie Thompson at the Wright Aeronautical plant in Phoenix, Arizona, about the problem. Charlie said there was a later, more efficient nose reduction gear (20:7) used in later models of the R-3350. This high ratio nose, Wright Model EA-2, had been used on the Model 1649 Lockheed Constellation. This was the last model 'Connie' built and the only one with that special nose reduction gear. It was never used on any other airplane. *Rare Bear* still wears that same nose gear.

The engine itself was a later version of the R-3350 that included an EA-1 power section (stainless steel cylinders and crankcase) and turbo compounding between the power section and supercharger.

Part of the weight reduction plan was in the propeller. Lyle located a lighter weight AD Skyraider prop with M20S-162-0 hollow stainless steel blades and a P-61 Black Widow spinner to replace the heavy DC-7 prop. With the stronger engine and larger propeller the blade tip speeds were important. The normal engine-to-prop ratio is roughly two to one—for one revolution of the engine the prop turns 0.4375 part of the circle. When the blade tips start to get up near the speed of sound, or at it, propeller efficiency falls off. The new engine-to-prop ratio was a slower 0.335. Although the changes did not show when the Bearcat sat in the pits, the crew anticipated better performance on the race course.

Joyce Shelton hoped her husband would relax once the airplane was flying and Lyle was actually racing. Instead, Lyle was spending more time at the airport and more money on the aircraft trying to improve its performance. He needed the first of many small loans to replace the blown engine in time to enter a race scheduled to be held in June, 1971, at Cape May, New Jersey. Lyle felt he was too close to winning to back off now.

In order to be ready on time for the Cape May race, crew members needed to truck the new engine to Stead and install it in the middle of winter. That would give time for test flights before they made the ferry flight to Cape May. Bill Coulter, a San Diego native, was also working at Aircraft Cylinder when Byard donated the R-3350 to Lyle. Coulter smiled a lot but he took his work seriously. He recognized part numbers for the pistons, rings, master rods, valves, etc. they needed. If someone brought the wrong one, he was quick to check their mistake. He helped Gregoire with the improvements and modifications to the hybrid engine.

Coulter and George Williamson fastened the new engine to an engine cradle on a small trailer they towed behind Lyle's half-ton pickup truck. In the bed of the pickup was a fully assembled Skyraider prop on a prop stand plus a drum of oil and some tools. They set off towards Reno following highway 395 north through the mountains of eastern California. An unexpected snowstorm caught them near Bridgeport, California. They were lucky when a snowplow came along shortly after they skidded a few feet off the road. The plow pulled them out, then cleared the road as it led them into town. Snow drifts, slippery roads, and traffic delays resulted in a 23-1/2 hour drive from the Aircraft Cylinder shop in Sun Valley to the hangar at Stead Field (560 miles) in Reno where the Bearcat was patiently waiting. Using a cherry-picker borrowed from the Nevada Air National Guard Coulter and Williamson hung the engine on the firewall on Sunday before returning to Compton. A few weekends later, after crew members were able to hang the propeller and connect all the systems, Lyle flew the Bearcat back to southern California.

Phoenix 1, the Bearcat's new name, was ready for Lyle to enter a cross country race from Milwaukee, Wisconsin to Alton, Illinois in May, 1971. For the ferry flight he used internal auxiliary fuel tanks to extend the range and planned refueling stops in Albuquerque, New Mexico and Kansas City, Kansas.

"During landing at Albuquerque my brakes went out. I borrowed a hangar there and spent most of the night repairing the brakes, intending to leave for Kansas City at dawn. I needed to be in Milwaukee by noon for the start of the cross-country race to Alton. It was barely light when I departed Albuquerque but before I left the New Mexico airspace my prop started going out. It was overcast down to the deck and I had no place to go. The engine started slowing down to 1400 rpm and I was slowly coming out of the sky. Fortunately I turned the plane towards Dalhart in the Texas panhandle. There was kind of a donut hole over the airport that was clear and I dropped right into the airport to land."

Lyle missed the start of the cross-country race and had to spend the day on the phone with the crew back at Compton telling him what needed to be done to get the prop fixed. He got some help from the local mechanics; the next day he flew directly to Alton to join Clay Lacy and Howie Keefe to watch the airshow. He left the Bearcat there for the next few days.

About a week later a tired Lyle returned to Alton to continue the ferry flight to Cape May. The Bearcat is a fast plane on the race course but it does not cruise fast. Lyle found that juggling his airline and air race schedules did not allow much extra time for just getting there and back. It was late afternoon when he left Alton and getting dark as he neared Philadelphia. Lyle discovered his electrical system was down and quickly radioed the Philadelphia tower.

"My exterior navigation lights have failed." he calmly explained to the tower.

""My TWA flights took me in and out of Philadelphia frequently. I am familiar with the layout of the field."

The controller quickly verified Lyle's ID, then gave him permission to land. It got so dark Lyle could not see his instruments on approach to the field. No problem for the former instructor who had shared solutions to unusual situations with the talented class of airmen a couple years earlier in San Antonio. He held a small flashlight in his mouth to see his instruments as he made an uneventful landing. Next morning he took off for Cape May.

When the racers got to Cape May they found a short course laid out partially over water. Little twelve to fifteen foot boats with people on board who served as pylon judges bobbed around in the water to represent pylons. Lyle qualified *Phoenix 1* in first place at 361.93 mph, followed by Howie Keefe in his P-51; Ormond Haydon-Baillie in a Sea Fury; Jack Sliker in a P-51; Ron Reynolds in a FG-1D Corsair; Dick Foote in a P-51, Leroy Penhall in a P-51; and Gunther Balz in a Bearcat. Two late arrivals, Clay Lacy and Len Tanner, both in P-51s, were allowed to race without qualifying because of the small number of entrants.

Lyle did not push his engine during the Friday and Saturday heat races, coming in second both days. Weather was good but speeds at this sea level airport were predictably lower than those recorded at the 5,000' altitude of Stead Field in Nevada. On Sunday, June 2, 1971, Lyle Shelton, *Phoenix 1* and the Bearcat crew enjoyed their first championship air race victory with an average speed of 360.15 mph over ten laps of the 7.25 mile course. Lyle's confidence in the Bearcat and the volunteer crew was confirmed.

"The biggest factor in our success," he said, "was the hard work of the crew." They were rewarded with the $7,000 first place prize. Most of the prize money was spent reimbursing the crew for their expenses. After reviewing their finances, Lyle and Joyce agreed they needed a sponsor or they had to confine entry into races held closer to home.

The Cape May race is remembered for the worst series of mid-air accidents in air race history. On Saturday, during one of the AT-6 heat races, a mid-air collision on the first lap destroyed one aircraft, fatally injuring the pilot. The second aircraft was severely damaged but able to land safely back on the runway. Two laps later another mid-air collision occurred with a third T-6 unable to avoid the flying debris. All three planes crashed and were totally destroyed. The three pilots did not survive. Professional Race Pilot's Association, FAA and New Jersey State Department of Aeronautics officials initially thought to cancel the rest of the weekend's races; after a lengthy meeting it was decided to let them continue. It was a bittersweet weekend for Lyle.

The ferry flight back to Compton took Lyle from Cape May to St. Louis to refuel. Albuquerque was the next stop. As he neared Santa Rosa, New Mexico the prop began going full fine pitch and the engine started running away.

"I was showing 3,000 rpm and I was pulling the throttle back to keep from overspeeding. I ended up running it idle at 3,000 rpm. When the airplane started coming down out of the sky pretty fast I was at 15,000 feet. The ground elevation there is about 7,000'. It did not take me long to get very low. I looked over at the interstate when I knew I was going to have to put it in. It was wide enough but there was too much traffic. I looked back towards this rolling pastureland and picked out a clear way and just put it right in out there in the boondocks. I rolled out, jumped a ravine, cut through and chopped up two barbed wire fences—rancher charged me $20 for repairs to each one—barely missed a couple of poles, and ended up rolling out on a fairly smooth rocky surface. Ran over and chopped down one mesquite tree which gouged the bottom of the fuselage. The barbed wire and cactus ripped up a little bit of fabric, but otherwise the plane was in pretty good shape. All the hydraulic oil that had leaked out of the prop was all over the engine and it was smoking quite a bit so I jumped out and got away from the airplane until I realized the smoke was from the hydraulic fluid."

A rancher who had seen the airplane going down pulled up in a pickup truck and drove Lyle into Santa Rosa to the bus station. He went to Albuquerque to catch a flight later that night to Los Angeles in time to get about two hours sleep before his scheduled TWA flight the next day. Lyle was calm throughout his ordeal. The smoke indicating a possible fire temporarily scared him. Otherwise he handled the situation the way he had been trained…and landed safely.

The Bearcat stayed in the New Mexico field for two weeks until Lyle returned with a replacement prop regulator. His old Brownfield buddy, R.L. McKenzie, met him at Santa Rosa and together they installed it. Then they borrowed an A-frame truck. Lyle lined out the area where he wanted to take off. He and R.L. pulled out stumps, mesquite trees, rolled boulders out of the way, filled in some holes, and made a rough runway. That took them all the afternoon. Next day they marked a temporary runway with pink toilet tissue—just pulled off strips to leave on the bushes—and Lyle was able to take off in a huge cloud of dust. After a routine refueling stop in Albuquerque he continued safely back to Compton.

The Bearcat and crew did not have far to go for the second 1971 race. It was a 1,000 mile event flown over a ten mile course (100 laps) at Brown Field near San Diego, California on July 18, 1971. The Bearcat qualified first at 324.3 mph, although nobody was worried about qualifying speed except for the starting position it earned. It was an endurance event for men and machines. For this race the Bearcat used two drop tanks from an A-4 Skyhawk for extra fuel. There were some impressive planes and pilots entered. Listed in the order in which they finished: Sherm Cooper in a Sea Fury; Frank Sanders in his Sea Fury; Darryl Greenamyer in a P-51; Lyle Shelton in the Bearcat; Gary Levitz with Vernon Thorpe as relief in their P-38; Gene Akers in a Corsair; Bob Love in a P-51; Howie Keefe in a P-51; Bob Guilford with Bob Laidlaw in relief in a Corsair; Wm. Jackson in a P-51; Leroy Penhall in a P-51; and Leo Volkmer in a TBM. Sherm Cooper won with an average speed of 330.1 mph; total winning time was 3 hours, 1 minute and 45.2 seconds.

The race was marred by a fatal accident on lap #80. Mike Geren pulled his Bearcat up off the course with horrified spectators watching as his plane erupted in flames and crashed into the northeast corner of the field. It appeared the master cylinder blew and the fire got into the accessory compartment and then quickly spread into the cockpit as he tried to land. Geren was not wearing fire protective clothing or gloves. It was not in common use among air racers at that time. Cliff Putman, George Williamson, and Lyle salvaged the airplane so they got a pretty good look at it. A vent—the eyeball vent—looked to be open when it should have been closed. If so, the fire probably got in through that hole into the accessory compartment and then right into the cockpit. Geren was probably disabled before he could land.

Lyle was having his own problems during the race. The drop tanks had changed his center of gravity and he was having a hard time controlling the Bearcat. He fell back when the regulator for the water injection system did not operate properly.

He said, "One of the most sobering moments in my racing experience was flying around a burning plane with a friend in it in the middle of the course. Mike was a TWA pilot and a good friend of mine. I remember while I was flying around the course I was thinking, 'I don't know what I'm doing trying to win this thing.' I pulled about 5" manifold pressure off the engine, cut it down about 300-400 hp and thought I'd just cruise to get through it."

The Reno National Championship Air Races were leading the way in promoting successful air racing events. Each year their attendance, number of entries and number of spectators increased. Prize monies lagged behind. The September, 1971, races featured top aerobatic stars: Bob Hoover; Art Scholl; Joe Hughes; John Kazian; Bob Herendeen; and others.

Sandy Sanders, who had been announcing the Reno races and air shows since the first one in 1964 had become popular in his own right. He described to newcomer and veteran spectators the aerobatic maneuvers, specifics about the race planes, and background information about the race pilots. He explained some of the rules governing pylon cuts, penalties, race horse starts, flying the course strategies, and even described some of the modifications made to familiar fighter airplanes to boost their speed and maneuverability. Sanders' enthusiasm contributed to the growing popularity of a few of the individual planes and their pilots.

Clay Lacy proposed an air race parade through downtown Reno on a weeknight to let the fans see the pilots and crews who worked on the airplanes. The parade, held on Friday evening, included racing airplanes in all classes. It originated at the Reno Airport, proceeded over Plumb Lane to Virginia Street, went north on Virginia past the blazing neon lights of the casinos where spectators lined the curbs, and then back to the airport. *Phoenix 1*, painted white with purple trim, was escorted by grinning crew members wearing matching purple pants and racy looking white jackets. (Purple pants for men were not readily available so Lyle's wife dyed some white jeans in her washing machine.) They looked pretty good parading down the street and purple became a popular color for the crew for the next several years. *Phoenix 1's* wings had to be folded to drive down the streets, of course, but the plane surprised many people by looking so much larger up close than it did on the ramp surrounded by P-51s and Sea Furies.

The week began with warm breezes and a sense of fun; it ended with snowflakes and controversy. There were ominous dark clouds overhead and snow showers just northeast of the course as the Sunday Unlimited championship racers formed up over Peavine Mountain. Temperatures were down in the 50s and dropping rapidly. The wind chill was in the 30s; winds were gusting 20 to 25 mph. Spectators who remained in the grand stands endured icy gusts of the west wind swirling around their legs from underneath the stands. Bone numbing blasts howled against their backs. Those lucky enough to have a blanket in their car huddled under it, sharing with friends, while they tried not to freeze. Fans were seen hurrying to stores in downtown Reno, some to Sears at Park Lane Mall and some to Penneys in the downtown area, to buy warm sweat shirts or jackets so they could stay and watch the Gold race. Some chilled spectators left for home. The die-hard fans stayed to the cold, bitter end.

The Unlimited pilots could see the flags over the grandstands whipping wildly about as they took off. It was a sign they were in for a bumpy ride. After take-off the race planes formed a line behind the pace plane, flew west to the back side of 8,266 foot Peavine Mountain, then turned towards Stead Field. When the pace plane pilot was satisfied the formation was ready, they heard the familiar "Gentlemen, you have a race!" Eager pilots pushed throttles forward as they roared "down the chute" at the east end of Stead Field. In the grandstands fans were on their feet watching for the first plane to dive onto the race course.

As the pack roared onto the course Mike Loening in his P-51 surged out in front. He immediately declared an emergency—a blown engine—before he completed lap one. During his landing down the runway, past home pylon, and in front of the grandstands, he discovered his hydraulics were gone, he was running out of runway, and there was a drop-off coming up fast. Bob Hoover was watching from overhead and warned Loening he had little runway left. Loening ground-looped the plane sending up a towering cloud of desert dust and weeds. He was unhurt but his beautiful P-51, *Miss Salmon River*, suffered major damage. The remaining racers pulled up during the emergency to allow room for the crippled airplane to land.

A protest filed by Lyle after the race claimed Greenamyer had failed to climb to the required 500 feet while the emergency was in progress. The Contest Committee agreed and fined Greenamyer $250 on each of three different violations. The Committee, however, did not disqualify Greenamyer from the race so he was declared the winner with a speed of 413.987 mph. Lyle was second with a speed of 413.066 mph. In October the PRPA's Board of Directors voted to suspend Greenamyer from sanctioned races for one year for unsportsmanlike conduct in not pulling up during an emergency, flying too low, and flying too close to the grandstands. A few weeks later the FAA suspended his license for flying outside the course and too close to the grandstands. Greenamyer challenged that claim and his license was reinstated. Reno Air Race Association suspended him from racing at Reno for one year. The incident resulted in frigid relations between Greenamyer and Shelton.

09

RECORDS AND RACES

In 1946, on a cold wintry day in Cleveland, Ohio, a Navy pilot flew a stock Grumman F8F in a near vertical climb to 10,000 feet in 98+ seconds. Since the Navy had not filed their intent to set a Time-to-Climb record with the National Aeronautics Association it was unofficial. It was highly publicized and generally recognized as the Record for Class C-1 airplanes (landplane, piston engine).

Winners of the Reno National Championship Air Races were not attracting sponsors. Some of the owners loved the challenge and excitement of the race; they had 'deep pockets' to keep them flying. Lyle, however, was using his salary and loans from the credit union. Rebuilding the wrecked Bearcat had depleted his savings. Air racing is an expensive sport. He knew he needed publicity---name recognition---to attract a sponsor. The Time-to-Climb challenge was one way to get noticed. After considerable research and planning for the flight Lyle practiced doing the climb in different segments so the engine would not be stressed too long at one time. To get a time on the first segment. he flew from the ground to 3,000 feet or 5,000 feet above ground level.

At another session he climbed from 5,000 feet to 10,000 feet AGL to get time and an approximate idea what angle of climb worked best. He set the power to the fastest allowable rpm at full throttle with water injection.

Lyle, Hickle, and Putman calculated the amount of fuel required—approximately ten to fifteen gallons. Finally, on a sunny day in February, 1972, they went to the Thermal Airport near Indio, California, for the challenge attempt.

Putman and Hickle made a device to hold the airplane by attaching a cargo release hook to the tail of the airplane.

Ready to Climb, 1972.
Shelton Collection

"We did not have the little tail cone fairing on there," explained Hickle. "The structure that the tail hook stops against was still there—in fact, it's still mostly there. We hooked the selectric release—pelican hook it's called—onto that. We did not know how we should anchor the airplane so we used a gas truck from the FBO at Thermal and dragged some concrete junk that had been stacked up at the back of the airport after something had been torn down. We piled up a bunch of this stuff in the dirt off the end of the pavement and then on the bottom we somehow wrapped a big chain or strap around the bottom chunk of concrete. Cliff stood off to the right wing tip giving hand signals to Lyle. They got the power up and when Lyle indicated he was ready to go he gave a signal, a kind of salute the pilots gave the LSO on catapult shots on the aircraft carrier."

At Putman's signal Hickle released the hook.

Lyle said he was initially shooting for a fifty degree climb. "I got airborne real quick, then as quick as I could I got the gear handle up, raised the gear, held the nose down and stayed low until the airplane approached 170 knots. Then I rotated so at a fifty degree climb angle I would maintain about 170 knots in the climb. Then I climbed up to about 3,500 feet AGL and hit a layer of warm air—an inversion out there—and the power dropped off so I had to drop the nose to around thirty degrees or so for about 2,000 feet of wet, warm air. Then I picked up the colder air again and raised the nose up at about 5,500 feet, back up to around forty degrees or something like that. At about 8,500 feet I just eased the nose gradually straight up so I went through the target altitude, 3,000 meters AGL (approximately 10,000 feet), just about vertical."

Two spotter aircraft circled at 3,000 meters as Lyle climbed vertically between them.

"The speed was dropping off pretty quick so I converted my kinetic energy at 8,500 feet AGL to climb energy but then the airspeed played out up around 11,000 feet. I was indicating about 60 knots and the airplane will not fly at 60 knots. I kind of went up like a dart, then sort of rolled it on its back and let the nose fall through. It straightened out like a dart. I was easing the power off, too. At 60 knots I eased off from about one G where the airplane would probably have stalled and spun, to about ½ G. We do not have a stall warning in the Bearcat. There is just a natural feel—a burble in the airplane—a normal stall you can feel on the stick and you know you are about to stall. I throttled back, left the engine at idle and came directly back down and landed."

It worked out pretty much the way it was supposed to. Lyle set the new Time-to-Climb record to 3,000 meters at 91.9 seconds. He was back on the ground in less than five minutes. The Bearcat and Lyle were comfortable together. He wasn't aiming to only fly fast…he wanted to test this machine---and himself--- to their limits.

At that time there were two sets of wings for the Bearcat. The standard long wings were used for the Time-to-Climb flight. Before the plane departed for the Reno races in September the second set of wings were clipped by about three feet reducing the total wing span to just over thirty feet. Richard Tracy formed new tips for the shortened wings from urethane foam. Initially he did not favor clipping the wing tips until his research convinced him the removed tips relieved the load on the wings in high G turns, made for a smoother ride as well as increasing speed on the straight-aways. Like the rest of the crew Tracy was working evenings in his spare time. When he had decided what material he needed for the modifications he went to a friend's dive shop. It was after business hours so he called the owner and got permission to climb over the fence and borrow some foam core board from which he designed the new tips. Then he had someone cover them with fiberglass. The first job was botched so he worked through the next night grinding off the old fiberglass and re-applying a new coat. He got bolts from a hardware store to attach new tips to the wings.

In 1972 Lyle and the crew mourned the death of Crew Chief Cliff Putman. Putman had joined the ranks of the T-6 racers in addition to his position on the Bearcat crew. In June he was killed in a T-6 exhibition race in Graham, Texas. Harry Smith was serving as crew chief when the Bearcat crew arrived in Reno in September They were also trying out a new name—*Phast Phoenix*—for the airplane.

There was no prize money for heat races in any of the classes when the race pilots arrived in Reno that year. Qualifying speeds determined which race and in what position each aircraft would start. The Unlimited Division was restricted to twenty entries with the top fourteen qualifiers flying in either the Consolation or the Championship race; the remaining six qualified for the Medallion race. Richard Laidley in *Conquest 1* headed the list followed by Clay Lacy, Lyle Shelton, Gunther Balz, Howie Keefe and Lloyd Hamilton. Greenamyer was sitting out his suspension.

Aircraft from all the classes flew over to Reno Municipal Airport on Friday afternoon and were hooked up to pickup trucks and towed over Plumb Lane to Virginia Street. The parade of airplanes, with pilots in the cockpits and crews marching alongside, proceeded along Virginia Street, under the "Reno, Biggest Little City" arch, then were towed back to Reno Cannon Airport on Friday evening. Fans greeted their favorite racers with cheers and toasts. Neon lights sparkled on highly polished airplane wings. Pilots waved and grinned. It was fun for all.

Saturday morning Lyle flew from Reno Municipal Airport to Stead Field, where he opted to go around the course a couple times before landing. Out on the back stretch the canopy locking pins gave way, the canopy twisted as it flew off, glanced off his face and knocked off the headset he was wearing; then it hit and dented the vertical stabilizer. He landed back on the main runway with an open cockpit and bruised and bleeding left cheek. The crew installed a stock F8F canopy borrowed from Bud Fountain. (A month or so later an air race fan, Ron Slaten, was hiking the hills, found the damaged canopy and returned it to the Bearcat crew.) The drag added by Fountain's high profile canopy reduced the Bearcat's speed in the Sunday Championship race. *Phast Phoenix* managed a second place finish of 404.703 mph. Gunther Balz in the P-51 *Roto Finish* was first at 416.160 mph. Laidley finished second but was disqualified for flying too low although he had been repeatedly cautioned over the radio during the race that he must fly higher.

Some pilots of the Unlimited Division considered forming their own group to promote air races. They looked for possible sponsors or investors but found no one willing to provide the necessary financial backing. Almost all the racers were finding the costs to maintain a racing airplane for only one appearance per year were prohibitive. Prize money was lower in the 1970s than it had been in the 1930s and 1940s. In 1938 Roscoe Turner earned $22,000 for winning the Thompson Trophy race. Gunther Balz, the 1972 Reno Unlimited champion race winner, earned $12,500!

Lyle was one of those whose expenses exceeded any prize money he won. Fuel prices were higher; repair parts were expensive and hard to find; hotels charged premium rates during race week so, with more crew members needed, his hotel bill sky-rocketed. Everyone needed bigger purses just to cover expenses.

It was obvious that one race per year in Nevada, however successful, did not give the national exposure needed to create interest in air racing elsewhere in the United States. Television coverage focused the public's attention on such events as the drama at the Munich Olympics when Palestinian terrorists killed eleven Israeli athletes. When President Nixon authorized the beginning of the Space Program stories about new frontiers in space filled pages of print media. Airplanes made the news when they crashed, not when they raced.

The members of the PRPA elected Lyle president of their organization in 1973 at a meeting they held at the first Miami Air Race. Clay Lacy, PRPA president for the previous three years, had approached Lyle about running for the job.

"I'd been helping Clay for the past year as unlimited representative. I was pretty ginned up at the time thinking this air racing thing was the wave of the future and we'll make a racing circuit here and make air racing big time. I was up at Clay's office in Van Nuys quite often while Joyce and I were still living near Long Beach. When I was elected president of PRPA I continued to use Clay's office in the Great Atlantic & Pacific Aeroplane hangar at Van Nuys Airport so I decided to move my family to where the action was. Joyce looked for a house in the valley and found one in Granada Hills."

The move to their new home lengthened Lyle's commute to work; however, one advantage of his airline pilot schedule meant no daily commute on the crowded LA freeways. He traveled at odd hours and could relax, enjoy the ride and listen to jazz on Long Beach station 88.1.

In a letter sent to members by PRPA in the early 1970s it described itself as "the only organization in the world chartered for and dedicated to the advancement of air racing—the world's fastest and most exciting motor sport. Its members are not only pilots, but mechanics, engineers, timers, (pylon) judges, administrators and publicists—all a vital part of the air racing community."

PRPA was founded by race pilot Art Chester in 1934, although it was not incorporated until 1939. Each class—Formula One, Biplane, AT6/SNJ, and Unlimited—was represented within the organization and was self-governing in matters pertaining to their group. A Board of Directors and Advisory Board assisted PRPA in broader matters such as developing and promoting additional air races. While he was president Lacy's input at various race sites was responsible for a high degree of professionalism and increased spectator interest in the sport. Lacy had suggested the Reno Air Race Parade, the prize for the best dressed crews, plus race course and rules improvements.

Lyle intended to continue Lacy's commitment to the growth of air racing, not a small task. It involved attending meetings with community groups in various areas of the United States where he explained the benefits of holding an air race at their local airport plus the requirements for the event. The job required research, discussion with potential participants, and many, many meetings. Bill Hickle, the new Bearcat Crew Chief, often had to make decisions on his own while the Boss Cat was looking for new territory for PRPA to conquer.

Aircraft Cylinder and Turbine Company had been generous with their support in supplying the Bearcat with engine parts, and sometimes an engine, starting with their first one in 1969. Although Lyle won the Cape May race that prize money barely covered expenses for the crew to make the trip from California to New Jersey. He was, therefore, extremely happy to welcome the US Thrift Association bank in Tucson, Arizona, as its advertising sponsor in early 1973. With that money in hand Lyle was able to enter the Miami Air Race January 16-21 at Miami, Florida.

Before taking off for Miami the crew finally solved a problem they had with the alignment of the air frame that prevented the landing gear from retracting properly. According to Hickle, the crew had strapped a pull ring in place to hold the cowl flaps in the retract cylinders. The problem existed from the start of the project and resulted from the crash landing at Valparaiso. There had been some pretty serious structural damage that prevented the wheels from properly aligning and locking when they were retracted into the wheel wells. When the big R-3350 engine was installed nobody realized how much air was going down into the landing gear area. A lot of air leaking from up around the cylinders back into the wheel well developed pressure on the wheels from the inside. It was keeping the gear from going up all the way. There was pressure on the wheels from the inside and they could not lock up properly.

The Bearcat always seemed particularly churlish when forced to fly long distances; its limited fuel capacity dictated frequent stops. Drop tanks were an option but slowed the cruising speed. After careful consideration and discussions with the crew, Lyle had internal auxiliary fuel tanks installed, making three stops to refuel along the route. Crew members flew commercially for this trip. Once at the Miami airport they recruited a few local mechanics to help. Most of the crew was on hand when the Bearcat touched down at the Tamiami Airport after an exhausting, but uneventful, flight from Compton.

After qualifying fourth, finishing the heat race second on Friday and first on Saturday, Lyle was overjoyed to cross the finish first in the Sunday championship race at 373.320 mph. He now had two first place wins, but not Reno—the big one. There were two big success stories here—the Bearcat win and the Miami race itself. PRPA members on the east coast had struggled for years to get this race going. Lyle congratulated them for a job well done!

Now Lyle was faced with the part of air racing he disliked the most—a ferry flight. Ferrying a racing airplane to and from various race sites was not a routine little jaunt. The engines take a beating during the race week, crew members are on their way home, weather can be a problem, and the pilot is already weary from the race week itself.

According to Lyle, "Flying those long distances back home is the hairiest thing we do. More so than the final race."

In 1971 he twice made unscheduled stops for mechanical problems enroute to Cape May and once on his return.

Cliff Cummins, a radiologist from Southern California, Lloyd Hamilton, a Pan Am pilot based at San Francisco Airport, and Lyle each had his home hangar in California so it made sense they fly back in formation from Miami.

When they took off there was a line of thunderstorms across the middle of Florida. They could not get through that line so they flew to the coast, then headed north following the Florida coastline. The Bearcat was leading the way as they let down under the stratus. As the ceiling continued to lower they went down closer to the water—about second or third floor height of the hotels they passed—flying in and out of intermittent light rain. Suddenly ahead they saw the towers from the Kennedy Space Center sticking up into the overcast. They quickly tightened up the formation and split the launch site right down the middle between those towers. No one seemed to notice so they continued on into Jacksonville to refuel. From there they headed for New Orleans, still under cloudy skies. Lyle switched from the radio frequency they were using to check their location with the closest airfield. When he came back on to talk to the other two pilots Hamilton was calling, "Hey, Lyle, come on back! Cliff is going down!"

Cummins' engine had failed and he was heading for a short little air strip somewhere west of Marianna, Georgia. Hamilton and Lyle landed at a small field about fifteen miles away. Cummins' engine had a broken connecting rod. He was unable to fly the plane home until he replaced the engine. Lyle had a scheduled TWA flight for the next day so he went on to New Orleans while Hamilton stayed to help Cummins. The Bearcat was parked at the New Orleans airport and Lyle hopped a commercial flight back to California. A couple weeks later he returned to finish the flight home by way of Brownfield, Texas to Albuquerque, New Mexico and then into Inyokern, California.

After the Cape May races in 1972 the Bearcat was moved to a hangar at Inyokern, Hickle's home. Hickle's brother and some local mechanics were recruited to help crew members Harry Smith, Pete Behenna and Bill Kientz prepare the airplane to challenge Jackie Cochran's 15/25 Km speed record.

On 12 December 1972 Lyle had received a letter from M. J. Randleman, Secretary of Contest and Records Board of the National Aeronautics Association approving sanction for the record attempt. Cochran's record of 464.374 mph was established at Indio, California in 1951. To set a new record Lyle needed to better that speed by at least 1%. Apparently the category was established in 1950 or 1951; there is no mention of this record in earlier lists.

NATIONAL AERONAUTIC ASSOCIATION
1025 Connecticut Avenue, N.W.
Washington 6, D.C.

RECORD CLASSIFICATION:	Maximum Speed Over a 16-Kilometer Straightaway Course Class C, Group 1 – Piston Engines.
DATE OF RECORD FLIGHT:	<u>9 April 1951.</u>
PILOT:	Jacqueline Cochran
AIRCRAFT:	North American F-51 MonoplaneIdent: N5528N
MANUFACTURER:	North American Aviation, Inglewood, California
ENGINE:	Packard Built 'Rolls Royce Merlin'Rated Horsepower: 1450
MANUFACTURER:	aircraft Engine Division, Packard Motor Car Co., Detroit Michigan
MEAN AVERAGE SPEED (TWO PASSES) OVER 16-KM COURSE:	747.339 Kilometers per hour 464.374 Miles per hour

s/C.S. LOGSDON, DIRECTOR NAA CONTEST DIVISION

Cochran had flown several passes over a 16 Km course, "beginning and ending at the northeast corner of the flagstone walk around the swimming pool at the Cochran-Odlum Ranch near Indio, California". Lyle wanted to attempt the record in the same area so he chose Palm Springs, California.

When Lyle called Jackie Cochran at the ranch and told her what he wanted to do she was all upbeat about it. Hickle did most of the work getting the course set up and the cameras and spotters in place. They invited Bob Downey to make the 15/25 Km speed run for the Class C-1A (Formula Ones) at the same time. Nicki Sparks of Omni Aviation Managers in Van Nuys had invitations printed and sent throughout the aviation community.

Fish Salmon, Cleveland era air racer and noted test pilot, was there as were many of Lyle's Naval Reserve friends. There were ads in the aviation newsletters to reach as many people as possible. A ceremony was planned to honor the MIA/POWs and increase public support and awareness of the many American military prisoners who were still unaccounted for in Viet Nam.

On March 3, 1973 Lyle, Hickle and the Bearcat were ready. A small area was set aside at the Palm Springs Airport for guests and spectators. A microphone was set up so Lyle could explain the speed run procedures. Then he made his comments about the MIA/POWs and asked for public support in locating these men and returning them to the United States.

"Jackie Cochran also gave a nice talk on the MIA/POW situation. She took up the cause real well," commented Lyle.

Cochran and her husband, Floyd Odlum, brought a luxurious RV to the airport. Odlum was seriously afflicted by arthritis; he spent most of his time inside the RV. Cochran mingled with the guests, renewing many old acquaintances.

The 15/25 Km course was set up to follow Ramon Road running roughly east to west from San Jacinto Mountain towards Thousand Palms over a 15.9 Km stretch. Lyle ran it several times. He experienced a problem with turbulence while turning around at the San Jacinto end. Both he and Downey, flying his Formula One, *Ole Tiger*, got a good shaking up. The Bearcat engine was running smoothly but Lyle was not getting the speed he needed from it.

"We ran back and forth and were not fast enough," Lyle said, "so I came back down and we started looking for the problem."

He and Hickle concluded someone inadvertently left a bolt in the air duct on the leading edge of the wing. When they cranked up the engine the air blew the bolt back down through the carburetor, down through the engine into the blower section where it hit the impellers spinning at 9,000 rpms, and there it damaged some of the impeller blades. By the time it got into one of the cylinders it was probably shredded into pieces. It damaged the piston in the cylinder it got into, then it spit it out of the exhaust. Once they found the problem they worked through Saturday night and on into Sunday to get it fixed. It was too late. The weather turned bad on Sunday and they were shut out.

A second attempt on the record was made at China Lake in May during the Armed Forces Day celebration. It was billed as part of the air show so Lyle got only one try at it .

He explained, "The cameras had to point up to catch the airplane at 12,000 feet. I did not have a compass in the airplane and was trying to get in the camera cone at 12,000 feet to 15,000 feet. The cone was narrow and the crew on the ground was trying to vector me—turn left, turn right—on radar but I could not get over the cone. On landing I lost a brake and ran off the runway."

The publicity generated by this record attempt did not attract sponsors. The Bearcat team worked hard to get the airplane to Reno and win enough money to keep them flying. After dinner at the Mapes, one of the crew members put a nickel in a slot machine, pulled the lever, and hoped for a jackpot. As they walked away empty-handed, Lyle chuckled, "Nice try.

Of the twenty Unlimited pilots entered in the 1973 Reno Air Races seventeen qualified. *U.S. Thrift-7-1/3 Special*, the Bearcat's latest name, set a new qualifying record of 426.602 mph. It won the heat race on Friday, then had a 'bye' until Sunday. It was perfect air race weather as the Unlimiteds—three Bearcats and four Mustangs—roared around the course with some of the sport's best pilots driving them. Shelton led Bob Love in his P-51 until lap 6 when Love's engine failed and he called a mayday. Lyle always described Love as "the best stick and throttle man in the business." He and Love were disappointed they could not duel it to the end. This fierce competition resulted in the Bearcat pushed to a winning speed of 428.155 mph, faster than his new qualifying speed record set a few days earlier.

As they watched the success of the Reno Air Races and the public's interest at Cape May, Lancaster, San Diego and Miami races several Unlimited and T-6 pilots decided to form their own company to develop and promote an air race. They named their company Air Race Management. It was funded by Lyle Shelton, Howie Keefe, Dick Sykes, LeRoy Penhall, Clay Lacy, Alice Rand and Omni Aviation (Nicki Sparks and Mike Eisenstedt).

The Mojave airport was a Marine Corps Air Base during WW II and was now part of the Kern County airport system. It had been the site of the 1970 California 1,000 Air Race. Its proximity to the Los Angeles area (approximately forty miles to the south) with two major highways—one east-west and one north-south—intersecting outside the high desert town of Mojave, made it convenient for fans to come up and go home the same day if they so desired. That was a plus as there were few motels in Mojave. The airfield lay just north and west of town assuring the promoters that a race course could be designed that would not overfly any populated areas. At that time Mojave was being used by several airlines who parked their out-of-service airliners on the field. There were also military ammunition storage bunkers scattered around the area. A few miles to the west loomed the rugged Tehachapi mountains.

With the help of Mojave Airport Manager Dan Sabovitch, Al Taylor, and the cooperation of businesses in Mojave, the first California National Air Race was held October 18-21, 1973. An Unlimited air race course generally needs a minimum of nineteen square miles of open space. This includes a buffer zone that separates the distance the race planes fly from the nearest spectators. Mojave easily met that requirement. Financing was a little tight but Air Race Management struggled to keep expenses under control. There were dozens of details to be taken care of: security of the field and planes; parking for fly-ins and automobiles; Sani huts; radio communications between police, fire and emergency crews and having those crews located in strategic places; first aid facilities for both crews and spectators; grandstands; concessions; ticket sellers/takers; adequate number of entry gates; parking directors; and on and on. These were not problems race pilots were used to handling before an air race; they had to do so for this one. A big problem that had plagued the Lancaster races also blew up at Mojave—the winds off the Tehachapis. Watching a Cessna 150 take off into one of the afternoon winds was heart stopping. The struggling little plane looked like it was going backwards! Gaining the altitude needed to fly westward into the headwinds to get over the Tehachapis was a battle of machine against nature. Sometimes nature won and the aircraft turned back to land and wait for calmer breezes.

The 8.206 mile course was closer to the grandstands than the course at Reno. To protect spectators the FAA decreed the Unlimiteds would fly the course clockwise instead of the usual counter-clockwise. After finishing third in the Saturday heat race the Bearcat flown by Bud Fountain suddenly exploded into flames. He crashed fatally at the northwest edge of the race course. Lyle was deeply affected by the loss of another friend to a flaming airplane. He felt it was imperative they mandate the use of protective gear for the pilots. During the following winter all four of the PRPA divisions investigated fire protective clothing for their pilots.

The Sunday Gold championship 8-lap race was another chance for Lyle and Love to go head to head. Bob Love was a crowd favorite since the 1964 air race at Sky ranch. He finished first that year but the complicated scoring system gave the win to Myra Slovak. Love was a tall, burly, platinum-haired man, quiet spoken, usually gentle-mannered. He was a fierce competitor; like most of the pilots he operated on the proverbial 'shoestring.' Lyle felt privileged to race against him.

Love forged in front from the very beginning with Lyle dogging his prop wash and waiting to make his move. He figured he could keep up with Love's Rolls Royce engine and still have enough kick to pass him at the finish. Whether he could was never answered. Love was forced by blower problems to call a mayday on lap 6. He landed safely. With Love out, Lyle was able to hold off the rest of the field to post his third win of the year at 396.614 mph.

Air Race Management did not meet expenses the first year. They gained a lot of experience, listened to a lot of gripes, suggestions and even some compliments. Attendance was not as good as they expected, probably because of events beyond their control. Early in 1973 the OPEC oil cartel had imposed strict export quotas on oil shipments to the United States. Gas prices shot up and long lines formed at gas stations as shortages resulted. By October consumers had learned to cope with the situation but the high price of gasoline discouraged many from traveling too far from home or to be stranded with an empty tank where stations reserved their supplies of gasoline for their local customers.

In retrospect Lyle felt 1973 had been pretty good to him: the derelict aircraft on which he and his crew of volunteers had labored over the past four years was the undisputed 'best' of the unlimiteds; and he had achieved his goal to be the fastest in the field. His first term as president of PRPA had been successful; he had been part of the inception of a new race series.

Air racing became a financial burden for Lyle. He had borrowed heavily to improve the Bearcat and invest in Air Race Management. Neither had returned enough to pay his bills. It stopped being fun and threatened the stability of his marriage. As U.S. military forces withdrew from Viet Nam Lyle hoped the country would return to normal and the excitement of air racing would attract a new generation of air race fans.

10

PROMOTING THE SPORT

In 1974 PRPA members reelected Lyle as president, two Unlimited races were scheduled, and Ed Browning of the Red Baron Flying Service, a Fixed Base Operator (FBO located in Roberts, Idaho), announced his sponsorship of the *Red Baron Air Racing Team*. Two airplanes, an AT-6 and a P-51, formed the team, each carrying the name *Red Baron*, the race number five, and using the same crew and pilot. Both the bright red planes were supported by a matching 48 foot trailer with *Red Baron* emblazoned on its side. The Unlimited Division welcomed this development as a good sign for the growth and financial future of air racing.

As president of PRPA Lyle found himself busier than ever. He spoke to town councils and chambers of commerce, showed slides and films, and answered questions to groups as diverse as members of the Civil Air Patrol in Indiana to executives of Grumman Aircraft Corporation in New York City. En route to an air race he made a quick stop at Castle Air Force Base in California to attend to a minor oil leak. The airport manager came out to talk to Lyle. He was interested in having air shows, maybe air races, when the airport would be under civilian authority. The downside was always the same…air racing is extremely expensive.

On a national scale media attention to air racing as a sport was poor. Air race results could not be found in the sports section of the newspaper, nor were they reported in the sports news on TV. In fact, it was hard to find air race results in either the newspaper or on TV. Potential promoters and sponsors were well aware of this lack of interest.

In early June spectator safety again became an issue when, after appearing in an air show near Sacramento, California, an F-86 Super Sabre jet failed to lift off in time while taking off from the field's short runway. It crashed into an ice cream parlor filled with families, exploding into a ball of flame killing the pilot and several children. National Transportation Safety Board hearings revealed the pilot, at a suggestion from the air traffic controller, took off from the short runway rather than waiting for clearance to use the longer runway. The public outcry about safety, warbirds, pilot inexperience, and air races (not involved here but included nonetheless) threatened the future of both air shows and air races. Without media coverage that highlighted the excellent safety record of the air races since their reappearance in 1964 promoter and sponsor interest lagged; new race venues withered and disappeared. To offset this public relations disaster air race promoters needed new ideas and new approaches.

It would be helpful, Lyle thought, to bring together pilots, crews, officials and PRPA associate members to provide an informal, educational meeting away from the pressure of the actual air race week. His secretary, Sandy Bloom, set up the first PRPA Seminar and Symposium in April, 1974 at the Mojave airport. There were clinics for timers, pylon judges, start/finish line flaggers, and ground safety personnel. Pilots met to discuss pilot procedures during an air race as well as various technical problems. The speakers for each of the clinics were active in their divisions. Participants came from all over the United States. Many had been to every Reno race held since 1964.

"How do we get GOOD publicity for air racing?"

Air racing was not classified as a sport by much of the media; it was also not considered newsworthy. Promoters and sponsors were not willing to invest enough money to run even or at a loss for the first couple years. The fledging races so far were badly under-funded. Participants in air racing spent enormous amounts of money for their aircraft, crews, and expenses during the year. Prize money was too low to keep them going.

" More races—a series of at least three for the Unlimiteds---are needed in various locations to broaden spectator interest. Volunteers are the key to keeping expenses under control," said Lyle.

Promoting air racing consumed much of Lyle's time. Attention to his airplane, his crew, and his family suffered. Morale in the hangar and at home declined.

One promising suggestion to widen interest in air racing was made by Clay Lacy during his tenure as PRPA President: invite air race fans to form local groups under the umbrella of PRPA. Lacy suggested they hold meetings, support local aviation events, volunteer to speak about air racing at schools, set up booths at local air shows, contact newspapers with stories featuring any local people who were involved. PRPA would provide continuing support with news releases and speakers. Working with Ken Carter and Don Ryder of Livermore, California, Lyle helped the first of these groups become a reality. PRPA provided addresses of its members in the San Francisco Bay area. Ryder and Carter mailed invitations to a meeting scheduled at the Holiday Inn in Livermore, California in August, 1974. The dozen people who showed up at the meeting became the nucleus of a group of dedicated air race supporters who decided on the name—Northern Area Group, Chapter 1 of PRPA. The group quickly grew in numbers. They volunteered to help with merchandise sales and distribute flyers at air shows, provide extra crew members to understaffed race teams, print an informational newsletter to members, etc. Eventually they changed their name to National Air-racing Group (NAG).

The 1974 Reno races got off to a fast start when Lyle and *Omni Special*, the Bearcat's new name, broke their own 1973 qualifying record of 426.602 mph with the new record speed of 432.252 mph. The much heralded *Red Baron*, piloted by Mac McClain, posted the third fastest qualifying speed, 417.330 mph. Lefty Gardner qualified the seldom seen P-47 belonging to the Confederate Air Force in Harlingen, Texas. It came in at 289.756 mph. It was slow but spectators were thrilled to watch this old airplane, whose shape was once compared to a Coca Cola bottle, flying the course. For once the fans were content to watch somebody fly an airplane low and slow The Reno skies were clear and temperatures mild; the crowd anticipated an exciting week.

During the winter the Bearcat crew had installed a P-51 spinner, metalized flaps, and experimented with nitrous oxide to boost the speed.

A lot of publicity preceded the debut of the *Red Baron Air Racing Team*. Roy 'Mac' McClain, an Ag pilot from Eufaula, Alabama, was race pilot for both planes. MacClain had won the T-6 championship in 1972. Sponsor Ed Browning was confident MacClain could also win the Unlimited championship in the soon-to-be modified red P-51.

There were seven starters for the Gold championship race on that clear, warm Sunday. McClain declared a mayday on lap 1, then quickly canceled it and rejoined the course. On lap 2 he called his second mayday and proceeded to land safely. The rest of the race was uneventful. Lyle thought he had a repeat of 1973 when he apparently finished in first place with a blistering 431.610 mph. Behind him Love's plane was trailing white smoke. As Love approached the finish line he pulled up high to set up for an emergency landing. After the race Lyle was notified he had been dropped to fifth place for not pulling up to 3,000 feet during McClain's mayday. The Bearcat's radio had been cutting out during the race and he had not heard the call.

"Through the years," he explained, "we have always had radio problems. We still have radio problems. In the early days we had cheap radios. With all the noise and vibration the Bearcat puts out, all that heat, it will burn up a radio or shake it loose. We just did not have a good radio and I lost communication."

The fans were puzzled about the penalty on Lyle this year for not pulling up for the mayday. There had been no penalty on Greenamyer the previous year in the same situation.

"The rules changed", according to the Contest Judges.

Bob Love was also penalized and dropped to sixth place when officials ruled he failed to complete the race by pulling up on the final lap. Third place finisher Ken Burnstine was declared winner.

Mojave's weather for the California National Air Races in October, 1974, was a race pilot's dream—calm, fair and warm. The spacious open field adjacent to the Mojave airfield was filled with dozens of general aviation aircraft---flown in for the day--- parked wing-tip to wing-tip. Some of the occupants camped under the wings of their planes during the races. Many arrived early in the morning before the airfield was closed for racing, boarded a farm wagon with hay bales for seats which shuttled them to the grandstands, and marveled at the vintage WWII fighters streaking around the race course. It was hot, dry, and dusty. Cold water was scarce.

Air Race Management's budget would only allow six or seven air show acts—good ones like Bob Hoover, Art Scholl, Frank Tallman, Lefty Gardner, Joe Hughes with wing-walker Gordie McCollom, Grace 'the Ace' Page, and the Bede jet trio in their Bede 5-Js. To keep the pace going ARM added exhibition Unlimited drag races and handicapped jet races to the program. The reaction from the spectators was mixed— "interesting", "exciting", "jets are boring", were a few of the comments. Friday's second unlimited heat race was canceled after a T-6 nosed over on the runway at the beginning of the T-6 drag race. The severely damaged plane had a bent prop and cracked crankcase; it could not be removed from the runway in time to resume racing that day. The Unlimited heat race was added to Sunday's program.

There were a lot of problems for ARM and its inexperienced staff to handle before this Mojave Air Race. "Where do we get cold water for people in the grandstands?" "Can't we get people through the gates faster? The lines out there are over a half-mile long!" "Spectators are walking out on the field from the other side. Where is our Security?" "Who's in charge of First Aid?" "Who is supposed to give out the VIP passes?" "Your wife is at the gate. Where is her ticket?" The list seemed endless.

ARM's staff was overwhelmed. They did not feel the results merited their investment in money and time.

Crew Chief this year for *Omni Special* was Bill Kientz. Hickle was in the hospital after an auto accident. Impatiently, Kientz waited in the pits for Lyle to discuss pre-race concerns and strategy. Exhausted, hot, and a little hungry, there was not enough time for Lyle and Kientz to thoroughly talk things over. It was somewhat of a relief for Lyle to climb into the cockpit away from the problems back in the office. That's what he was here for...to race his Bearcat!

Eleven Unlimiteds started in the Sunday championship race, the most ever for a single race at Reno or Mojave in this class. The pilots had complained all week about the difficulty in seeing the pylons. On Sunday at least half of them were charged with one or more pylon cuts.

The race pilots agreed they needed better designed pylons and more practice time available to become familiar with the course.

The Bearcat started the race in first place and led the field the entire ten laps—or so Lyle thought. He never saw McClain pass him.

"I thought it was the easiest race I had ever won. I even throttled back on the last lap. I lost sight of McClain and when I did see him up high I thought I had lapped him. I was back at about 45" (manifold) and 2200 to 2300 horsepower. The crew really chewed me out on that one."

McClain said he let Lyle set the pace, maintaining a close distance slightly higher and waiting to make his move. On the final lap, when Lyle throttled back McClain suddenly dove down and flashed by the Bearcat to take the checkered flag. His winning speed was 382.207 mph; Lyle's speed was 381.719 mph. Lyle had been looking for the flag, saw it and thought it was for him. He was stunned when his gloomy-looking crew told him the surprising news. The crew had been unable to get the radio working so they could tell him McClain's position. One crew member suggested—playfully—a rear view mirror be installed.

Despite the ideal weather Mojave's attendance was down from the 1973 figures. Timing of the event might have been the reason; Los Angeles Dodgers were playing the Oakland Athletics in the World Series from October 12-17. TV ratings went through the roof in Los Angeles but attendance at the air races suffered.

Events in 1975 varied only slightly from 1974: Lyle was re-elected president of PRPA; a second Air Race Symposium was held in March at Mojave Airport; and Lyle took second place in the June races at Mojave when Cliff Cummins zipped by the Bearcat at the finish line to win. Cummins' speed was 422.000 mph; Lyle's second place finish was 421. mph. It was almost a photo finish. Lyle was almost too embarrassed to face his crew.

Pilots and owners in all classes were scrambling to find new ways to make their airplanes fly faster. Engineers and designers who worked for major airplane engine or related parts manufacturing companies were recruited to modify stock WW II fighters into air racers. Few owners had money to sponsor these projects but there were lots of potential crew members with the necessary skills willing to volunteer as mechanics and technicians. Competition between teams was intense.

Until now no airplane underwent as radical a change to its appearance as the *Red Baron*. It arrived this year with two sets of propeller blades, one behind the other, each rotating in the opposite direction--contra-rotating propellers. They were formerly installed on a British Beverly Blackburn bomber during WW II. Some engine and airframe modifications to the airplane were necessary, of course, but nothing was so startlingly visible as those twin props up front. It was a challenge to the other unlimiteds and they knew it.

Grumman Aircraft maintained a field service support facility at China Lake near the Inyokern Airport. Lyle's highly modified Bearcat, a Grumman product, attracted some of the plant mechanics who volunteered to help Hickle and his brother, Art, with ongoing work.

Because Lyle was not always available to test the airplane the Grumman workers recommended a local pilot who had flown Skyraiders in Viet Nam and would be available to fly the Bearcat when needed. His name was Jim Pate, the first pilot other than Lyle to fly his plane. Pate did a pretty good job handling the eccentric airplane; he made good landings and didn't let it backfire a lot it when it started. Lyle wanted Pate to do some aborted takeoffs—that is to get up to speed and then chop the throttle and directionally control the airplane to a stop.

"This was a maneuver I learned during advanced training in Corpus Christi. There were no two-seat Skyraiders so they did several aborted take-offs before making their first flight."

Hickle recalls one day, "It was just before we were going to Reno. Pate was doing a power ground run when he nosed the airplane up. It got the prop. I was standing off the wing tip and as the prop hit the concrete hot pieces of metal and concrete were spraying over me. I was not hurt but we had to rush around and get another set of blades from Wally McDonnell. We got the blades to the prop shop and they got them fixed and back to us in time for us to get to Reno. And we did good."

The marginal weather—alternately cloudy and rainy, then warm with partly clear skies—did not seem to dampen the spirits of better than 62,500 spectators during the 1975 Reno Air Races. However, it did squeeze the qualifying schedules of all classes. By Friday the weather was no longer a concern.

Since 1972 when Formula One pilot Tommy Thompson suffered an apparent heart attack on the back stretch of the course and crashed fatally during a race the Reno races and air shows had been fatality free. On Friday both those records were shattered.

At the start of a heat race M.D. Washburn, a popular T-6 pilot, appeared to cut in too quickly around pylon one. His left wing collided with the pylon throwing him out of control and into the ground. Washburn died on impact. Air race officials decided to continue the day's schedule with memorial tributes to be planned for Saturday or Sunday. They launched a between-races air show act with Joe Hughes flying his 650 hp Stearman inverted with wingwalker Gordie McCollom on top attempting to pick up a ribbon which was suspended between two twenty-foot poles. As they neared their target a sudden wind shear pushed the Stearman---still inverted---to the ground damaging the vertical stabilizer and killing McCollom instantly. Hughes was somehow able to roll the Stearman upright and landed safely. Some of the shocked spectators left the grandstand in tears. Pilots and crews mourned the loss of the two men. They paid tribute to their skill and courage. They continued flying.

Sunday was a great day for an air race with fluffy white clouds scattered across the brilliant blue Nevada sky. Greenamyer, who earlier in the week set a new qualifying record of 435.445 mph in *Conquest 1*, had the pole position. As they waited to take off his prop governor failed and he could not start. Jack Sliker, winner of Saturday's Silver race, took off immediately as alternate. Cliff Cummins was first to mayday when he burned a piston, then landed safely. Next to drop out was Ken Burnstine in his colorful P-51 when his engine backfired. It blew out the induction system, with the blast tearing out parts of the air scoop and cowling and sending them tumbling to the ground. He, too, landed safely. Lyle held the lead for all eight laps, winning with a speed of 429.916 mph. He collected first prize of $11,967. The *Red Baron* finished second.

There was still another tragedy in 1975. On September 16, on his way home to Wadley, Georgia, Jack Sliker crashed fatally while attempting to land for refueling at the Flagstaff, Arizona, airport. When the 1975 Point Champions were announced in November it was no surprise that number one was Lyle Shelton with 15,618 points. Jack Sliker was second with 10,642 points.

11

He Fell Out of the Sky

At the beginning of 1976 the PRPA members adopted a new name—
United States Air Racing Association (USARA)—and elected Don
Beck president. Lyle was freed from some of the administrative duties
that had kept him so busy the past three years. He was still deeply
involved in the Air Race Management group promoting Mojave races
and the annual symposium. He also wanted to challenge one or two
speed and altitude records.

In 1969 Darryl Greenamyer, flying *Conquest 1*, had wrested the 3-
Km speed record for piston engine propeller driven aircraft from the
Germans when he set a new record of 483.041 mph at Edwards Air
Force Base, California. The Bearcat crew agreed they could do better.
Lyle reserved June 12-13 from the National Aeronautics Association
to challenge Greenamyer's record at Mammoth, California. Because of
insufficient time to set up all the necessary timing systems to make the
record internationally recognized, Lyle re-set the new date in August.

The Mojave Airport hosted the first air race of 1976. Before all the
contestants checked in tragedy struck. On Wednesday as Ken Burnstine,
winner of the 1974 Reno races--- was approaching the airport, his P-51
Susie Q went out of control and crashed, killing him on impact. Burnstine
was scheduled to appear as a prosecution witness in a drug –related trial
later in the year. Rumors swept the air racing community about the

possibility of sabotage to his airplane to prevent him from testifying. Investigations followed but nothing was found to support that theory.

In 1976 Hickle was still recovering from his accident and not able to work full time on the crew. Some work was done by new volunteers. The aircraft was repainted white with a three-tone purple stripe down the side and renamed *Spirit of 77*. One of the new volunteers recommended changing the carburetor air system where they sucked air in through a duct straight down into the carburetor. They were already using a down draft carburetor but changed to an inlet engine air duct on the top of the cowling with a scoop in front of the canopy. Lyle worried that the duct was too light weight for the kind of speeds he was running. He was busy with his regular scheduled TWA airline flights.; there was no time to test the new modifications before they left for Mojave. It was no surprise when a minor problem delayed their qualifying run from Friday afternoon until early Saturday morning.

Before the qualifying run at Mojave the crew temporarily hooked up some oil lines with hose clamps.. Hose clamps were used in some places on the engine but on the big, heavy oil lines they usually used big fittings. For the qualifying run the crew thought the clamps would hold. They didn't. When the Bearcat throttled up and headed down on the course to qualify the oil hose came loose. The next seconds were tense as the engine seized and Lyle struggled to get the crippled Bearcat lined up for the runway. As spectators and crews in the pits watched helplessly a black plume of oil streamed out behind the plane. Pilot and plane plummeted like a rock towards the hard desert floor. The pits were silent except for the fire engines, sirens screaming, that sped along the runway. At first there was no sign of the gear, then the tail wheel appeared and the gear doors opened. It was too late. The gear never fully extended and the Bearcat made a three-point landing—two prop tips and the tail wheel. A shower of sparks followed the plane as the prop tips ground along the tarmac. The stunned spectators thought the plane was on fire. Then relief swept over the crowd as those closest to the runway shouted, "There's no fire! No fire!" The shower of sparks followed under the plane as Lyle struggled in the cockpit. He had little control as he slid over 4,000 feet down the runway before coming to a stop. Fire crews immediately surrounded the plane and sprayed it with foam to make certain there were no lingering sparks or flames. Lyle, shaken but unhurt, climbed down from the plane and walked away. The Bearcat fuselage was wounded; the propeller blades were ruined. The estimated cost to replace them was $7,000 to $10,000. The engine was not repairable. Estimates were upwards of $35,000 to replace it.

3-pt Landing at Mojave, 1976.
Bill LeSanche

That evening Bearcat crew, friends, and spectators gathered at dinnertime at White's Café in downtown Mojave. When a dejected Lyle walked into the café he spoke to no one. Several people invited him to join them but he declined, then he turned, went out the door and trudged slowly down the street to his motel room. He didn't remember going to the restaurant, or walking back to his hotel room. It took him awhile to face reality....he was broke and so was his airplane.

The rest of the planes were on the course racing the next day while Lyle and Pete Behenna took the bent prop and seized engine off the Bearcat, loaded them onto the pickup, and drove back to Van Nuys.

The four propeller blades were useless for an aircraft. Instead they became art objects. Mike Klarfeld, one of the volunteer lawyers working with PR PA at the time, got one of those grotesque-looking blades, had it chromed and mounted on a stand in the corner of his office. Lyle still has one blade in his garage. He thinks the other two were sold by an aviation-oriented shop called *Nostalgic Aviator*. The headless Bearcat remained in Wally McDonnell's hangar at Mojave until the following spring.

Mac McClain and the *Red Baron* won the 1975 California National Air Races.

An alleged violation of procedure in the Formula One class during the Mojave races erupted into a major upheaval within USARA. As vice-president Lyle found himself caught up in the problem. Over the next few months he attended many meetings with representatives of each racing class trying to resolve the problem of standardizing procedures and penalties dealing with rules violation, especially in the direction of granting to those accused of a violation a fair and impartial hearing. At a general membership meeting held at John Ascuaga's Convention Center during the Reno Air Races in September tempers flared, shouting, booing, and finally some walkouts seemed to indicate the end of the organization as it had existed since the 1930s. When tempers cooled negotiations began between the National Air-racing Group and the United States Air Racing Association to address the issues and to unify the two groups. Although Lyle was not racing he kept in touch with those members working to solve the problems until a resolution was reached in 1982.

Getting the Bearcat ready for the 1976 racing season and challenge to the 3-Km speed record had cost Lyle a considerable amount of money. As the dismal year ended he had no desire to go air racing again. He declared he was "burned out." Without prize money or sponsorship he did not get the Bearcat into the air for almost four years.

In 1989 when Lyle spoke at the NAG banquet he was asked, "What was the biggest factor that kept you from winning after 1976? What was the biggest stumbling block?"

His answer: "Lack of preparation. Guys having to make a living and coming over to work on the airplane at night when they were tired and for no bucks. I had no money to buy good material or to have a good place to work. All this amounted to was a bunch of guys just flailing about trying to get the airplane where it was flyable, get it up to Reno. Every heat race at Reno for years and years I did a test hop, trying to figure out things during a heat race. With an airplane like that trying to run 125 knots to 140 knots faster than it originally ran you've got to have professional preparation. You've got to have planning, a budget—a BIG budget—and that's it. We were ill prepared for Reno every time we went there."

The man who wanted to go faster than everyone else now couldn't race. He had no money. His airplane was completely disabled. His spirits were low. But he wouldn't sell the Bearcat. It sat in the corner against a chain link fence, at the Van Nuys airport, for almost four years as a constant reminder of what it had been and what it might become again—the fastest airplane on the course.

12

STARTING OVER

The job of getting the Bearcat fuselage from Mojave to Van Nuys Airport was assigned to Lyle's teen-age step-son, John Slack, a high school student in Granada Hills, California. This was the outgoing teen-ager's chance to prove he was maturing into a responsible young adult. John recruited ten people to help and mapped out the route with the fewest obstructions. It was no small task.

At the start of his summer vacation, John took Lyle's white El Camino pick-up truck to Mojave and drove around looking for the best route back to Van Nuys. At first he thought he could tow the airplane down highway 14 to clear the mountains, then get off on side streets and into Los Angeles county but Kern county permits to travel major routes were too expensive. After about a dozen trips looking for other routes on all the back roads Wally McDonnell told John he had towed an F9 Panther out of Mojave on Silver Queen Road. It was a dirt road, 25 feet to 30 feet wide, that had been used when power lines were erected in that area. It was pretty smooth and went all the way up through the hills. It came out by Willow Springs raceway in the Rosamond area and ended at the L.A. county line. John talked to L.A. city officials about using back roads in the county and they gave their OK. He drew a map and time schedule to meet county officials at the Kern county line. They would guide the convoy through some of the more congested areas.

Slack used a 1960 Chevy ½ ton pickup truck to tow the airplane. They took the bed off and constructed a mount that held the tail wheel. Then they lifted up the tail of the airplane and bolted it inside of the mount, positioned the fork on top of the mount, and folded the wings. That's the way they drove it down to the Van Nuys airport.

They had a 20-foot Ryder box truck leading, with a 'Wide Load' sign up front, driving in front of the wing tip side so cars would be avoiding the truck and not hit the airplane. The pickup also had 'Wide Load' signs on its front and the rear of the airplane. The following truck also had a 'Wide Load' sign on the rear and was positioned so no one could come too close behind and hit the airplane. The convoy left Mojave around 4:00 p.m. In order to avoid commute traffic on the Sierra Highway they went over Old San Fernando Road, Balboa Blvd, Renaldi, and onto Havenhurst until they reached the Van Nuys Airport gate about 6:00 a.m. Their only mishap occurred when they side-swiped a fence and damaged a flap.

The airplane sat on the truck at Van Nuys airport another three weeks, then it sat next to the fence until they started working on it in late 1979.

Getting the Bearcat from Mojave back to Van Nuys had not been easy; John was very proud of himself for solving the big and small problems. Lyle was impressed

In the years after his retirement from the Navy Lyle kept a hectic schedule with PRPA, his TWA schedule, and improving his racing aircraft. After the Mojave incident he had no money to repair the plane. He was restless on his days off between his TWA flights. Joyce had hired a yard man to keep up with the garden. Lyle was not good at and did not enjoy doing handyman work around the house. He felt compelled to be flying some kind of airplane so he looked around for something that would suit him. In 1962 he had done agricultural spraying in the Texas Panhandle and it appealed to him. It was only a short step to get a formal checkout as a sprayer. He responded to an ad in the newspaper *Trade-A-Plane* placed by an Agricultural Pilot training center in Casa Grande, Arizona. He enrolled in their program and was soon on his way to South Dakota for his checkout with his ground and flight instructor, Bill Kelly.

Kelly was short and stocky and looked like a prize fighter rather than a pilot . He had watched Lyle race at Reno in 1975. When the application came in for training from Lyle Shelton, Kelly told his boss, "I'll be his instructor." Students started out in a Super Cub, however, Lyle was qualified to fly the 'Thrush", their advanced sprayer. It was too cold in South Dakota to spend much time training with water in the sprayer so the training moved to Casa Grande, Arizona.

Because of Lyle's experience as a Navy flight instructor the company decided to start an agricultural aviation school separate from their spraying operation. Kelly operated the school in South Dakota and Lyle trained students, especially those qualified for the GI bill, in Arizona. He invested some borrowed money to become half owner in the Ag Pilot School at Casa Grande and traveled all over the United States recruiting students. One trip took him to Washington, D.C. to investigate getting foreign contracts to train students from overseas. When Lyle was off on his TWA scheduled flights his partner ran the school. Their goals and methods of conducting business differed and their relationship became strained. Finally, during the Arizona State Ag Association convention in Casa Grande Lyle and his partner had their final confrontation. After two years in business together the partnership ended.

Kelly's weathered face was split by a big grin when he showed up in Van Nuys some time later. The two pilots toured the area, inspected the Bearcat, and shared a drink or two at the local pub. In the ag spraying off-season, Kelly was a long-haul truck driver. He volunteered to do some driving should Lyle ever need him. A few years later Lyle called him for help.

After the agricultural aviation school venture ended Lyle invested in the air cargo business. He and a partner founded Sun Fest Airlines with their headquarters in Las Vegas. Initially they used a Piper Seneca and a Piper Lance to transport canceled checks from a bank in Las Vegas to the Burbank Airport. The checks were picked up there by courier trucks and immediately driven to the Federal Reserve Bank in Los Angeles before the start of the next business day. They began to do a lot of overnight work for photo labs as well as carrying other light cargo. Soon they were running five aircraft. As they expanded their routes and type of cargo Lyle took out a second mortgage on his house to invest in the business. Problems began when they could not find mechanics to do the required aircraft maintenance on schedule. One FAA inspection showed some required maintenance had not been done at all, which started, as Lyle says, "giving me some grief." Once again he found running the business needed a full-time manager to keep up with the daily problems. Lyle's partner brought a third man into the business. They soon took over the bank contracts Lyle had developed and started a separate company for themselves. Lyle was leasing two of the airplanes so he turned them back. He just folded. The whole deal probably cost him $100,000 before it was all over. He was losing as much money in business as he had in air racing, and not enjoying it one bit.

In September, 1978, Chris Wood went to work as a mechanic for the Great Atlantic & Pacific Aeroplane Company at the Van Nuys Airport. The shy, good-looking young man saw what appeared to be a derelict airplane sitting on the edge of the field, got the wild idea that he might be able to buy it, restore it, and then maybe race it! Airplanes had fascinated Chris Wood from his early childhood in Pomona, California. He was more interested in the construction of the aircraft than in the flying of them. It was only natural for him to graduate from the Northrop Institute of Technology with a degree in Aviation Maintenance.

Wood was not alone in his interest in the Bearcat. A co-worker, Bill Noctor, also had dreams of buying, restoring, and racing the former champion. Noctor's aviation background included the Naval Aircraft Electrical School in Florida while in the Marines. He, too, graduated from Northrop Institute of Technology and was now working for the Great Atlantic & Pacific. He was a quiet, lean man, smiled easily, and thought it might be fun to approach the Bearcat's owner to work out a deal.

After the pair contacted Lyle they found the 'derelict' Bearcat was far more valuable than anticipated. They couldn't afford to buy it. When Lyle mentioned he would like to restore the airplane, Noctor and Wood were interested and quickly volunteered. Planning started immediately. Starting work had to wait for the money. Starting the cleanup was the first step.

The staff of Air Race Management asked Lyle to run the Mojave races October 27-29, 1978. Some of the former ARM crew and volunteers responded to Lyle's call for help. This year ARM presented the crowd with drag races and relay races in the different classes. Even crop dusters raced. Sky-divers raced in the only direction they could—down. The colorful T-6 Condor Squadron from Van Nuys put on their act. And a B-25 made a simulated bombing run. Steve Hinton, who had won the 1978 Reno races in September, notched his second win of the year at Mojave.

"It was far more difficult to be running the races on the ground than flying the races in the air," said Lyle.

In February, 1979 the long awaited International Air Race and Show was held at Homestead General Airport, Homestead, Florida. It was an Unlimited class only event organized and promoted by Don Whittington. The airshow included the Acrojets, Red Devils, Bob Hoover, Frank Sanders, and the Confederate Air Force's 'Tora, Tora' Tora' routine. Author Martin Caiden did fly-overs in his beautifully restored JU-52 *Iron Annie*. The short 7.0 mile course made pilots work hard for their wins. They had to fly fast and tight around the pylons. A $150,000 purse guaranteed significant prize money available for heat races and finals. Steve Hinton, the Gold race winner on Sunday, flew away with $20,000!

There were other pilots who coveted the 3-Km speed record that Lyle wanted to challenge in 1976. (*Listed by the National Aeronautic Association as "International Record: Class C, Group I [Airplanes with Piston Engines], Speed in a straight Line.*). The latest to announce an assault on that record was Ed Browning, sponsor of the *Red Baron Air Racing Team*. Greenamyer's record stood at 483.462 mph. To achieve a new record the new speed must be at least 1% better. Steve Hinton was chosen to fly the *Red Baron* P-51 over the measured course laid out at Mud Lake, Nevada, in August, 1979. Actor Cliff Robertson was invited to supervise a film special of the attempt. Over the week the team spent at Mud Lake they broke Greenamyer's record but did not break the 500 mph goal that Lyle was aiming for. On August 14, 1979, the final day of the NAA sanction, Hinton and the *Red Baron* set the new speed record at 499.018 mph. Many in the aviation community felt that was as close to 500 mph a propeller driven airplane could reach.

When the Reno races were run in September, 1979, Hinton had engine problems with the *Red Baron* during the championship race. He completed the race behind the winner, John Crocker. Hinton immediately declared a mayday. As he tried to set up for his emergency landing his engine seized, the propellers stopped propelling and became huge air brakes dragging the airplane down to the desert floor. From the grandstands all that could be seen was a column of smoke rising from the wreckage.

Sandy Sanders sadly reported, "It looks like we have lost Steve Hinton."

What followed is legend in air racing history—Steve Hinton survived! Pieces of the *Red Baron* were scattered for yards across the sagebrush but when rescuers reached the scene they found Hinton alive, still strapped in the cockpit. The fuselage had separated and rested several yards away from the burning wings. Hinton recovered from his injuries and was flying airplanes within a year. After the fire there was not enough left of the *Red Baron* to restore it. Browning had spent over $300,000 modifying the airplane; it was a total loss but its short, illustrious career encouraged several newcomers to try for new levels of excellence in air racers.

Although the price tag for air racing was steadily increasing Lyle was determined to find the money to get the Bearcat back in the air. He wanted to race again!

Work on the Bearcat didn't actually begin until sometime in 1979. The props and engine were a total loss after the 1976 spectacular landing at Mojave. There was very little money for the project so work was done as parts became available. Piece by piece and part by part, Chris Wood, Bill Noctor, John slack, and Greg Shaw were transforming the derelict back to its racing form.

Now there were other concerns—about the status of air racing itself.

13

IT WAS EASIER THE FIRST TIME

At the beginning of 1980 the outlook for air racing was grim. The 1980 Mojave races were canceled. An Unlimited race scheduled at San Marcos, Texas in July was canceled. A major shake-up in the Reno Air Race Association management left doubts about past agreements with race pilots. At a RARA Board of Trustees meeting in February they voted to fire Jerry Duty as Race Director. No reason given. General Floyd Edsall, formerly in command of the Nevada Air National Guard, was chosen to replace Duty. The pilots were happy to hear Edsall promised to work closely with pilots in all classes. John Lapham was removed as Chairman of the Board and replaced by Thorton Audrain.

Bill Jones of Aircraft Cylinder Company provided an R-3350 engine for the Bearcat that summer. The work pace accelerated. The crew set its goal to fly in the Reno races in September. During the day the Bearcat sat in an Omni Aviation Insurance Company parking space. In the evening it was moved inside the Greater Atlantic and Pacific Company hangar. Mel Gregoire and Mac McKinney supervised modifying and installing the engine. New Hamilton Standard M20A-162-0 Skyraider propeller blades were balanced and installed. The Bearcat looked the same as it had in 1976 – white background with purple trim down the side – the purple rainbow. John Tegler suggested a new name – *Rare Bear*. Time ran out before testing was completed; Lyle would flight test the plane when he ferried it to Reno.

Early in the morning of September 8, 1980, two excited young men set out from Van Nuys airport in a rental truck headed for Stead Field. They quickly left the Los Angeles traffic, drove through Antelope Valley and climbed towards Reno on Highway 395. They did not talk about the spectacular scenery as they skirted the eastern edge of Yosemite Park; they talked about cylinders and pistons, oil pressure and superchargers – in short, an airplane engine. Their arrival in the pits at Stead caused a lot of surprise. Those who were aware of the work being done to restore the Bearcat gave them little chance of finishing in time to fly this year. It took the arrival of *Rare Bear* the following day to convince everyone that the "Bear Is Back!". As Lyle arrived and flew high over the field Slack and Wood were amused to hear some spectators identify the aircraft as a Skyraider, based on the sound of the big R-3350 engine.

The seventeenth annual Reno Championship Air Races began on September 9 with three days of qualifying followed by racing on Friday, September 12-14.

Besides the personnel changes in RARA's management, there were big changes on the field. The biplanes were gathered in a hangar instead of tying down on the ramp. In a large hangar next door were the Formula Ones. The public could watch the mechanics inside the hangars working on the little planes; they could not go inside the hangars. The airplanes and their crew were protected from the gusty winds and unexpected showers that had tormented them in earlier years. The ramp from the East to West was separated into three areas: air-show performers, T-6 air racers, and Unlimited aircraft. The Unlimiteds were each assigned to 40' x 40' pits to park the aircraft and any support vehicles they might bring with them. Special passes were required for private vehicles to park or drive in the pits. Crew members were issued special identification that allowed them to accompany the aircraft out on the taxiway for run-ups or when lining up before their race. Spectators were now charged a daily entrance fee to wander freely in the pits or to sit along the flight line to watch the races in progress.

As soon as it became obvious Lyle was serious about returning to air-racing there was no shortage of volunteers to work on *Rare Bear*. As it had happened before, there were some who came to work one or two weekends and then expected their expenses to be paid during race week. Joyce, who was handling the book-keeping chores, had to protest considering everyone who had put a wrench on the engine as a true crew member entitled to a paid trip to Reno.

There were several welcome supporters visiting the pits and anxious to see the Bearcat back in the air: Lyle's Aunt Irene, her husband Floyd, and Pete Harris were there every day. Harris could be seen beaming with pride as he watched Lyle climb up on the wing and into the cockpit to taxi out for take off for each race. Aunt Irene was busy taking pictures to show to the folks back home in Brownfield, Texas. If Lyle had concerns that he and *Rare Bear* were not fully ready for this race, he didn't show it.

When *Rare Bear* lifted off to make its qualifying run, Lyle faced a formidable lineup of competitors, some of whom had emerged in the five years he was absent from racing at Reno. The speed to beat, 421.607 mph, was set by Don Whittington in his P-51 *Precious Metal*. *Rare Bear's* rookie crew was very pleased their plane qualified at 402.752 mph on their first outing.

The lack of time to thoroughly prepare and inspect, tweak and tune, haunted Lyle in Friday's heat race. As Unlimiteds approached the field in formation he had a fine spray in the cockpit. When he tried to declare a mayday, he found his radio was not working. He landed and returned to his pit. Repairs were made but things did not get better on Saturday. His blower system failed on lap 1 and his engine blew. He made his landing look routine, but he was finished racing for 1980. There was a chance of rain predicted for the Sunday Gold race. As far as the *Rare Bear* team was concerned, it had showered all over them on Saturday.

Mac McClain won the Gold race in #69, *Jeannie*, at 433.010 mph, a new race record.

When the government sold the Stead facility in 1967, 3,500 acres were bought by Bill Lear, the prolific inventor who had developed the Lear Jet airplane. Lear built hangars and workshops at Stead where he intended to develop a steam powered engine for automobiles and busses. He was also working on a new airplane with a composite fuselage. The steam car project was abandoned but at the time of Lear's death in 1978 the Lear Fan prototype was nearing completion. Several members of the *Rare Bear* crew visited the Lear Avia hangar each year to see the progress of Lear's last dream. Before he died in May, 1978, Moya Olsen Lear promised her husband she would "Finish It". Finally, in December 1980, it was ready for test flights. Because of a contract stipulation with the Irish Government --- they were going to subsidize production of the airplane in Ireland ---the first flight had to be made in 1980. Dozens of people lined the main Stead runway on Tuesday, December 29, to watch the unfolding of another page in aviation history.

As so often happens to big projects small details show up and delays occur. Minor glitches delayed the takeoff of the Lear Fan for the next three days. An overheated brake and blown tire on the final day, December 31, seemed to end all hopes. Nevertheless, on January 1, 1981, the runway was lined with people waiting for Lear's Chief Test Pilot, Hank Beaird, to lift off. When the graceful white airplane rotated a flood of emotion was unloosed in the spectators. They could not contain their grins, tears and hugs. Many of the watchers were Lear Avia employees who had worked long and hard to see this day. The seventeen minute flight ended successfully. A government official dated the certificate December 32, 1980! The Lears had always been generous supporters of Lyle and his team; the team was delighted to see Lear's last dream fulfilled.

In August, 1981, after months of negotiations, the National Air Racing/International Formula One group and the United States Air Racing Association, split since 1976, agreed to participate in each other's events and to have all such events sanctioned by USARA. The proposed agreement would be submitted to the memberships of both groups for vote of approval by the end of the year.

The Reno Unlimited race course was professionally surveyed in 1981. The official length was determined to be 9.273 miles around. Questions arose about the accuracy of measurements in the past years and the accuracy of qualifying and race speeds as a result. Since all contestants were clocked based on the same course length there was no doubt about the winners, only their official speed.

After the 1980 blown engine *Rare Bear* remained at Stead Airport until a new engine was installed in August, 1981. Lyle brought the plane back to Van Nuys for some work but time was limited and so was testing. When he landed back at Stead in time for qualifying the 1981 races in September the only visible change was the solid purple striped down the sides of the plane replacing the purple rainbow.

Rare Bear qualified sixth at 416.037 mph and won the Friday heat race at 416.721 mph. Lyle was experiencing some problems with the water cooling system that got worse during the Saturday heat. He declared a mayday and pulled up high off the course to lose some of the speed he had built up so he could position himself for his emergency landing. With smoke trailing behind him he touched down, rolled safely to a stop and waited for the dejected crew to retrieve him. The problem could not be fixed before Sunday but they promised to be back next year.

The 1981 Unlimited race ended with Skip Holm in Jeannie winning at 431.29 mph.

Off the course and away from his hangar Lyle had worked hard trying to unify the air racing divisions back into one group. He firmly believed a unified air racing group would lead to better and more air races. The situation improved in October when the International Formula Midgets and the Formula Ones did merge and become the International Formula Ones. With all the racing classes now autonomous Lyle hoped the two umbrella groups, USARA and NAG, could work out their differences and again discuss a merger.

14

Almost There

Rare Bear remained at Stead Airport until March, 1982. A ferry engine was installed so Lyle could fly back to Van Nuys. Lack of money again forced Lyle to postpone work on the airplane until more funds were raised. Crew members mounted a campaign to raise money directly from Bearcat fans by advertising in aviation newspapers and the National Air-racing Group newsletter. Their donations were much appreciated---and needed. Work slowly resumed.

Dave Cornell, one of the mechanics who had been working with the crew since 1979, helped Gregoire rebuild the supercharger to improve its efficiency. Mel was near retirement from Aircraft Cylinder. He had heart problems that were becoming worse while he worked around the massive engine, inhaling fuel and oil fumes. During the past few years he had researched superchargers. He was anxious to try some innovations that he felt would give better performance to the engine . Cornell, young and eager to meet the challenge presented by the big hybrid engine, was an experienced aircraft mechanic. He researched old operating manuals to look for ideas that had been tried and succeeded in the past. Now he and Mel were ready to apply their ideas to the big R-3350.

Dave still lived in his parent's old home in the San Fernando Valley ---not too far from the Van Nuys airport. He had added a workshop in the huge backyard where he worked at his own pace. His wife Bonnie had room to raise her pet goats. In this peaceful setting the two men worked together towards their shared goal…more speed for the Bearcat.

The *Rare Bear* crew installed a new Skyraider propeller. Weight reduction measures included removing part of the hydraulic system and some heavy non-structural components from the airplane. The white with purple trim paint scheme remained the same. An addition was a large, menacing-looking bear crushing an airplane – suspiciously resembling a P-51 – painted on the vertical stabilizer

Summer flew by as Lyle watched the busy crew spend hours preparing *Rare Bear* for its next race at Reno.

RARA celebrated twenty continuous years of air racing in September, 1983. They gave the fans more for their money by adding Thursday to the schedule as a race day. The fans were assured of plenty of exciting races when it was announced thirty-one Unlimiteds had entered; twenty-eight had qualified. A sobering note was the report that Mac McClain had succumbed to cancer in February.

Crowds of air race fans celebrated in the evenings. The hotels and casinos were full; the spectators were making merry, wandering down Virginia Street from the open doors of one noisy casino to the next. Several former members of the Bearcat crew came by the pit to renew old memories and wish *Rare Bear* a victory in the Sunday race. Lyle greeted them looking relaxed and happy. The crew looked neat in their white tee shirts emblazoned on the front with 'Lyle Shelton's Rare Bear'. Joyce found a small, striped umbrella to mount over the cockpit to keep it cool until it was time for the pilot to climb in.

There was a poem lettered on the cowling of *Rare Bear*:

> *a saddle on a motor*
> *burning dynamite for gas*
> *with a little lifting surface*
> *as will hike it off the grass*
> *3000 leaping horses*
> *with a feather for a girth*
> *500 miles per hour*
> *50 feet above the earth*
> *the breed of man who rides her*
> *is an optimistic guy*

with magic in his fingers
and a telescopic eye

When the races started the weather was good, the spectators lively and cheering all their favorites. As the Unlimiteds taxied by the grandstands for the first heat race on Friday, hundreds of sentimental fans were cheering the return of *Rare Bear*.

Sylvia Sweeney noted in the National Air-racing Group's newsletter, *NAG RAG*, "Lyle is Keeper of the Faith – and without question the Magnificent Underdog. No matter what he will do his best to blast by every plane in the sky. Which is exactly what his fans are waiting for. Is this the Year?"

No, it was not. Of the seven Unlimited aircraft that came screaming down the chute and onto the race course on that windy Sunday, three were destined not to finish the race. Lyle's competition was awesome! Neil Anderson in Sanders' Sea Fury *Dreadnought*; Rick Brickert in Frank Taylor's P-51 *Dago Red*; Ron Hevle flying Destefani's P-51 *Strega*; Don Whittington in his own P-51 *Precious Metal*; Destefani in his second P-51 *Mangia Pane*; and Lyle in *Rare Bear*. *Strega* pulled out before officially starting lap 1. Positions changed as the remaining six planes roared around the course. *Dago Red* pulled up and out on lap 5.

Although Lyle did not know it yet, *Rare Bear's* trim tab had been rigged wrong giving him a lot of nose down trim. He could not make a tight turn because of the stick force. He fought to keep *Rare Bear* on course but was judged to have cut the deadline, disqualifying him. That was not the only problem. His water injection system malfunctioned and a cylinder was overheating due to a fouled sparkplug. Lyle pulled up and set up for an emergency landing. The winds were shifting but he planned for a southwest wind as was indicated on the surface. He was also getting a tail wind back out over the hill.

"I ended up high so I slipped it to get down on runway 14. As I came out of the slip the chopped wings did not cushion it like I had been used to with the long wings so I landed hard and blew a tire."

Neil Anderson in *Dreadnought* won the Gold race with a rather sedate speed of 425.24 mph.

The merger between NAG and USARA was formalized in April, 1984. A joint operating committee was selected to oversee the transition between the two groups. An election was scheduled for later in the year to select a new name, with all members asked to submit suggestions. Although Lyle was no longer involved he was relieved the organizations were finally unified.

Rare Bear was out of action, still resting next to the Lear hangar at Stead, when an Unlimited air race was held in Moose Jaw, Canada, in June, 1984. Twelve Unlimited pilots and planes made the long journey to participate in the race which was won by Skip Holm in Joe Kasperoff's P-51 *The Healer* at 359.152 mph. The race was exciting and well-received by spectators but the promoters lost money. Financial support could not be found for a second event. Once again the lack of sponsors and the high costs of air racing kept the sport from growing.

Rare Bear spent another lonely winter at Stead; however, it did attract a new friend who would play an important role in the Bearcat's future. His name was John Penney.

Penney, Lear's new Director of Flight Operations, was in an office overlooking the parking lot where *Rare Bear* rested. He first watched it race in 1980, then again in 1981. As he watched he decided he really wanted to be part of the team. He got Lyle to autograph his log book and later Penney introduced himself, offering to help where he could. He did not expect to fly *Rare Bear* but it was a thrill to be part of the effort.

After the emergencies in 1981 and 1983 Penney came out and hung around with the crew, loaned them his old blue station wagon, helped out in the pits when he could doing things like standing on his head in the cockpit bleeding the brakes for the guys.

"I probably did about four years of helping out before I actually got to operate the airplane," he recalled.

Lyle learned that Penney was a test pilot for Lear as well as an F-4 Phantom pilot in the Nevada Air Guard and realized he might be the right man to have as a backup pilot. At the same time Penney prepared a resume for Lyle asking for a spot on the team as spare pilot. It was kind of a mutual thing. He preparing to give Lyle his resume the same day that Lyle said he was flying an awful lot and would like Penney to come on as a spare pilot.

Penney was certainly qualified to take on the enormous challenge of flying a hot airplane like *Rare Bear*. His youthful looks and serious demeanor did not fit the stereotype of a devil-may-care pilot. He did fit the image of 'test pilot'. An Air Force Academy graduate he is type rated in the Lear Jet, Air Transport Pilot, single and multi engine land planes. He has flown T-6s, P-51s, A7Ds, RF4s, the Lear Fan 2100; he is active in the Nevada Air National Guard with the rank of Major. Penney learned to fly in a Piper Cub in 1961 so he was familiar with tail-draggers. He was inducted into the Quiet Birdmen (QBs) and into Mensa International. His responsibilities as test pilot for the Lear Fan give him the experience to communicate with the ground crew regarding the pertinent engine readings they need to pinpoint problems in the big radial engine.

With *Rare Bear* just a few feet away Penney could go out and sit in the cockpit to familiarize himself with the controls. The engine was not on the plane but Penney visualized the engine start, take-off and landing. Lyle gave him copies of the Grumman manuals on the Bearcat and soon Penney knew everything about the airplane.

It was over six months before the crew could get *Rare Bear* back in the air so Lyle could ferry it to its hangar in Van Nuys. Before it left Stead Lyle had Penney practice aborted take-offs but Penney did not fly *Rare Bear* until June, 1985. It was several more months before Lyle could get a new engine for *Rare Bear* so it missed the 1984 Reno races.

In March, 1985 the National Air-racing Group newsletter, *Professional Air Racing* (formerly called *NAG RAG*) announced a new air race would be held June 1-2 at Minter Field, California. The field is located eight miles north of Bakersfield, just off the main north-south route 99, which made it convenient to the huge southern California area. Though Bakersfield itself lacked the entertainment possibilities of Reno its nearness to Los Angeles did make it possible for spectators to drive up for the day.

The event got off to a troubled start when the planes tried to qualify on Thursday and Friday. The course overflew cotton fields in which laborers were working until 5:30 p.m. The FAA would not give clearance for the race planes to fly until the fields were clear. Spectators who expected activities to begin at 4:00 p.m. had to wait until after 5:00 p.m.

By working long hours the crew was able to install a surplus Air Force engine in time for *Rare Bear* to enter the race. Lyle flew to Bakersfield and challenged some of the recent Reno champions – Ron Hevle in *Strega*; Steve Hinton in *Super Corsair*; Skip Holm in *Stiletto*; John Crocker in

Sumpthin Else; Frank Sanders in *Dreadnought* ; Del Williams in *Mangia Pane*; Howard Pardue in his Bearcat; Lloyd Hamilton in *Baby Gorilla*; John Putman in *Coyote*; and Frank Sanders' second 'no name' Sea Fury. Hevle finished with the best qualifying time, 431.451 mph. Lyle was third with 418.774 which placed him in the Gold heat race on Saturday.

When the planes came down on the course for the Saturday race *Rare Bear* was trailing the field. He quickly moved up, passing Crocker, Holm and Hinton. Hevle managed to stay out in front winning the heat at 402.962 mph with Lyle in second place at 399.048 mph. The stage was set for a fast, exciting air race on Sunday.

The eight-lap Gold race around Minter Field's 9.281 mile course was close and exciting. *Rare Bear* was at the back of the pack because of pitch instability problems at the start. Lyle overcame his problem then was able to come from the back of the pack to finish second, passing everyone except *Strega*. The crowd was on its feet cheering for the *Rare Bear* to win. The Bear was running fast but not handling well. After the race Lyle said he experienced some extreme porpoising due to the pitch instability (caused by aft CG conditions), something that needed to be corrected before Reno.

On Monday after the Bakersfield races Penney finally got his chance to fly *Rare Bear*. He flew one flight around the area to get better acquainted with the plane, landed, gassed up, then flew on down to Van Nuys. It's a good thing the flight was not ten minutes longer because Penney had a problem with the bearing in the blower. It was just about ready to seize. The entire bottom of the airplane was covered with oil when he taxied to the hangar in Van Nuys and shut down. They had to take the blower off, trash it, and replace it. The blower section was eating itself. Penney kept the blower drive main gear as a souvenir. It was heated up so much it turned steel blue.

"I'm going to turn it into a lamp base one of these days," he said.

Fewer than three months remained before the Reno races. The crew replaced the supercharger, then discovered a problem with a main crankshaft bearing that required a complete engine change. That required more money and more time. Penney's experience as a test pilot was helpful to the crew in pinpointing some of their problems but they were not able to complete the changes until the beginning of race week in Reno. Once again the flight from Van Nuys to Reno was considered a test flight.

Flying *Rare Bear* presents the pilot with new and different experiences. In the traffic pattern his nose is much higher than it would be in a stock Bearcat. Some of the crew had Penney believing *Rare Bear* was a demon and he would be operating right on the edge—"If I touched one thing wrong the airplane is going to fall over on its back. Except that there are no flaps and the wings are clipped so you have to fly a faster final approach and the nose is up where you can't see the runway very well the airplane really handles very well."

A record thirty-five unlimited planes entered the Reno Air Races in 1985 Entries included an astonishing nine different types of WW II aircraft: seventeen P-51s; six Sea Furies; four Corsairs, and one Super Corsair; two Bearcats; one Skyraider; one B-25; and one Douglas B-26. This display of classic aircraft was a feast for the eyes of those strolling through the pits. In the air the sights and sounds were awesome!

Spectators were surprised when *Rare Bear* appeared Tuesday afternoon at Reno with John Penney as pilot. As a rookie he had to fly with the Unlimited check pilot and get a quick briefing before rounding the pylons. There was not much time to become familiar with *Rare Bear* on the course but he put on a good show by qualifying seventh at 429.485 mph. It was cold, wet and windy as Penney took off for his heat race on Thursday. He did not push the engine hard, but enough to stay in front and win at 407.502 mph. Things were looking good in Friday's heat until the fifth lap when an oil plug worked loose. The oil drained out as Penney deadsticked in to a safe landing. The crew found the culprit was a pre-oil plug which was safety wired to itself and not to the engine. It was a surplus engine that was purchased from the Air Force test lab. Had the team installed the plug the Q.C. (quality control) procedures they had instituted a month earlier would have prevented such a happening.

Even with a spare engine it would have been nearly impossible for Crew Chief David Cornell and the crew to change the seized engine overnight and be ready to race on Friday. That left the crew sitting in the pits as Steve Hinton won the Gold championship race on Sunday flying the Planes of Fame's *Super Corsair* to the winning speed of 438.186 mph.

The aviation world was shocked and saddened on Monday after the races when news reports announced that veteran air show performer Art Scholl was killed while filming a pilot's eye view from his cockpit for the movie Top Gun. He went down over the Pacific Ocean about twenty miles north of San Diego. A popular performer at Reno since 1979 he also did stunt flying in more than 100 movies and TV shows. He was mourned in the pits by his many friends in all classes – pilots and crews.

15

Welcome Jack De Boer

John Penney announced in the January, 1986 *Rare Bear* newsletter, *Bear Facts* "Lyle has allowed me the freedom of establishing a team structure which several of us feel will enhance our competitive success. The organization features some very clear cut lines of responsibility and authority. It is not our intention to turn this into a military organization, but with as much work as we will have to do in the near future, it becomes imperative to formalize the structure of the team so that everyone involved understands where their responsibilities lie."

Penney also stated, "In the past, even with the invaluable support of many individuals for things such as engines, pumps, paint shops, parachutes, radios---and more---the fact remains that there has been a continuous drain from the pocket of the man who owns this plane to keep it flying. This will no longer happen. Either the project will be self-sustaining through sponsorship and winnings, or there will be no racing for #77."

The remainder of the newsletter outlined the details of the program, including a Table of Organization chart. Despite Penney's denial, some crew members grumbled the plan sounded "too military."

For Lyle the figures had added up: the operating crew had worked about 40,000 hours since 1969, not including about 8,000 hours of his own time. They were fortunate that many thousands of dollars had been contributed by past and present supporters.

"That is a hell of a lot of work!!!---and fun, and joy and tears, and thrills, and terror, good luck, bad luck, feuding, friending, loving, instant aging stomach lining---and the rest. It takes a long time to get a good crew together," declared Lyle.

Tired of mortgaging his house and borrowing money from the Credit Union to finance his passion for air racing, Lyle hoped Penney's more organized approach to running the team would keep expenses in check.

Early in 1986 Dr. Richard Tracy contacted Jack DeBoer, whom he had met during the 1985 races, suggesting De Boer might enjoy sponsoring a race plane---specifically #77 *Rare Bear*. DeBoer was owner of the Residence Inn chain of hotels. He was also an active private pilot with a ticket to fly Lear jets. He had a large hangar at his headquarters in Wichita, Kansas where he kept his Lear, two Gulfstreams, and an AT-6 in the process of being restored. DeBoer loved airplanes! Tracy forwarded the promotional package full of pictures, past records, and crew profiles to acquaint him with the makeup of the *Rare Bear* team, their experience, and their commitment to the goal of winning. Conversations and negotiations took place between DeBoer, Tracy, John Penney and Lyle. Past experiences has shown Lyle he was not good at negotiating the details of contracts and other business matters. Tracy and Penney reviewed DeBoer's offer and explained it, as best they could, to Lyle. They agreed it sounded good and there was a potential for further financial help if this year worked out.

In late July DeBoer agreed to a limited sponsorship for one year. With money to buy parts and only a few weeks before the races, Crew Chief Dave Cornell and the crew began preparing the *Rare Bear* for competition. This included replacing the old M20A-162-0 blades on the Skyraider prop with H-20G-162-0 blades and working full time to complete the race engine at Aircraft Cylinder and Turbine.

It was a major setback when Mel Gregoire, chief engine mechanic, had heart surgery and was unable to work with the crew for several weeks. With Gregoire unavailable, crew members spent five days installing new Simplex rings and making adjustments on the shiny new engine with the bright yellow power section casing. Tests were done on the stand

and looked OK. In August, 1986, the engine was trucked to Stead where *Rare Bear* had remained since September, 1985. The engine was installed on the airplane and Penney flew it back to Van Nuys. While aerodynamicists Tracy and Carl Friend supervised some tuft tests of the airflow along the fuselage; testing was also done on the new propeller and water injection system. They were out of time when Penney left on Sunday afternoon in September for Reno.

Temperatures were in the 90s when race crews arrived on the ramp at Stead to get settled in their pits and ready for qualifying to begin on Monday. Already in a pit next to the flight line and ready for the challengers sat *Rare Bear* with its new paint scheme using DeBoer's corporate colors – cream with copper frost and navy blue accents. The Residence Inn logo was prominently displayed on the sides of the fuselage.

Photographers were overjoyed late Sunday afternoon when John Sandberg's long-awaited new homebuilt race plane named *Tsunami* (Japanese for tidal wave) touched down for the first time at Stead. There was a big crowd and a lot of stop watches along the flight line when pilot Steve Hinton went out on the course to qualify that week.

A cold front moved in on Monday with temperatures dropping rapidly and brisk winds swirling over the course. Lyle and Penney decided to get *Rare Bear* out on the course for a test run and have Penney check out pylon placement. He was not out there for long. A newly installed piston ring broke sending shredded metal through the engine. Penney was able to make a successful emergency landing and the crew spent a few minutes feeling utter despair as they sat quietly inside their rental truck.

"Not again", despaired Lyle. "We've got to get it flying so we can qualify by Wednesday afternoon. Let's get busy."

They diagnosed the problem to the Simplex rings they had put in the cylinders.

The idea was to keep the cylinders a little bit drier; to try to keep oil from getting up into the cylinder. When oil gets up into the combustion mixture it lowers the detonation threshold so it's easier to get the engine to detonate. The Simplex rings wiped the cylinder walls drier so they could run higher power without worrying about detonation. It appeared the Simplex rings worked too well. They kept the cylinder walls so dry they actually caused one of the cylinder rings to weld itself to the cylinder

Remove Engine, 1986.
Bucky Dawson

wall and it broke off. When they popped the cylinder the engine was junk. The crew resolved that if they could find a new engine they could remove it and install the new one in time to qualify.

The *Bear* was towed down to Al Redick's Classics in Aviation hangar where the crew ducked in out of the raw wind and hunkered down to regroup. The challenge was daunting: find a new race engine, remove the useless old engine, install new engine, and qualify by 5:00 p.m. Wednesday evening – a mere forty-eight hours away. New sponsor Jack DeBoer was scheduled to fly into Stead when the field re-opened to general aviation traffic Wednesday evening. DeBoer's automobile license plates bore the message 'Can Do', his own personal motto. The crew decided they could do it. After scurrying about the Unlimited pits to locate someone who could lead them to an available Wright R-3350 engine, Frank Sanders, owner of *Dreadnought*, agreed to let them use a stock R-3350 he had 'in the can back at Chino.'

John Slack, with one volunteer helper and two peanut butter sandwiches to sustain them, left Stead by truck about 10:00 p.m. Monday. The young volunteer was awfully quiet as he and Slack headed south from Stead, through Reno, Carson City, and the foothills beyond. He finally asked, "Where are we going to get the engine?" A surprised Slack replied, "It's at Sanders' hangar in Chino. But we have to go to our hangar in Van Nuys first to pick up the trailer with the engine cradle."

At first the young man remained silent, then he whispered, "My wife will kill me." They were too far into the trip to turn around so a phone call to the wife was made, the situation explained, and the urgent journey continued.

It was 465 miles to the team hangar at the Van Nuys Airport. They picked up a trailer with an engine cradle mounted on it, sped 70 miles over to Chino airport, and loaded up the Sanders engine early Tuesday morning. Often Lyle cautioned his step-son to 'take it easy on the gas pedal' when Slack took the car out. For this trip it was 'drive careful with that engine'.

It was barely light when the two young boys climbed over a fence at the Chino airport to get to the Sanders hangar With the help of an early bird they located the engine, managed to get it mounted on the engine cradle, find a restaurant to get enough food to get them through the long trip back to Stead and be on their way. They towed the trailer back up the narrow, winding highway 395 through mountainous eastern California and back into Nevada, arriving at Stead Field Tuesday evening about 9:00 p.m.

Rare Bear owner and its spare pilot had retired to a quiet motor home near Redick's hangar. They marveled at the determination of the crew. They stayed out of the way while discussing their options. It was soon clear the crew would get the engine off and be ready to install the new one when Slack returned. Would the exhausted crew be able to hold up long enough to get the new engine hung, systems connected, and a couple run-ups to test it before the deadline! Lyle realized this was expecting a lot from his group of volunteers but over the years they had already accomplished small miracles. He believed they 'can do'.

There were a lot of eager mechanics from other crews who volunteered to help the *Rare Bear* crew that night; few had experience on a radial engine…especially one as highly modified as this one.

"We want to see you in the air so we can beat you," boasted one mechanic from a competitor's team.

During Slack's marathon trip the crew removed the damaged engine from the plane, then detailed the systems while they waited. They worked in shifts. There were crew members sleeping in the back seats of cold cars and crew members sitting on the chilly concrete hangar floor with backs against the wall as they napped. A race fan, Somers Blackman, who happened to have some tall spotlights and an outdoor heater in his truck ready for delivery to a customer, came by to offer their use.

The crew from one of the Formula Ones went to a fast food restaurant to buy hamburgers and hot coffee, their treat, for the tired mechanics. Tools were borrowed, needed parts were contributed. Al Redick offered the use of his heavy equipment, without which the job could not have been done. They worked throughout the cold Monday night and all day Tuesday.

Penney and Lyle were on hand when Slack arrived back at the hangar Tuesday evening; seventeen hours remained before the Wednesday 5:00 p.m. qualifying deadline. The crew had to install the engine, hook up all the systems, re-hang the prop, tow the plane out on the ramp to do ground run-ups on the new engine, then turn it over to Penney to qualify.

When *Rare Bear* was towed out late Wednesday afternoon, the tense, tired faces of the crew showed both optimism and anxiety. A large crowd of spectators and crews from other race teams were cheering as *Rare Bear* took off eight minutes before the newly extended 6:00 p.m. deadline, rounded the pylons, waggled its wings, and qualified at 402.171 mph on a totally new engine with no time on it. Penney ran the power setting given to him by the crew chief with no problems noted.

When the sandy-haired, six foot four DeBoer and his crew touched down in his Gulfstream jet at Stead later that evening they were greeted by cold, blustery weather and an exhausted, exhilarated 'Can Do' Bearcat crew.

During the heat races Penney was able to keep the engine speeds at a fairly moderate level while breaking it in. On Thursday he flew the six-lap race to second place at 398.032 mph. Friday he inched the speed up a little to finish second at 419.783 mph.

On Saturday, with slower competition, he finished first at 406.565 mph. Lyle watched anxiously from the pits.

The new engine was working fine but it was not broke in enough to push it to the limits. When Penney and Lyle discussed their options they favored a conservative approach. If they could finish this race and take the airplane back to Van Nuys for the crew to work on the new sponsor might under-write some much needed improvements before the next race season. And so Penney went conservative. With the tense crew down on the ramp watching *Rare Bear* banking around the pylons, Penney and Cornell communicated air to ground as they cautiously tested different engine settings. Penney stayed in the air long enough for them to get some preliminary readings.

On Sunday when he turned on the nitrous the engine started to shake really bad. There had been problems with Y-leads—the spark plug wires. When they get old and break down they cannot run the proper amount of electricity through the leads. The pressure in the cylinder gets so high there is not the proper amount of power across the spark plug.

The crew discovered this later on. When Penney switched on the nitrous there was more cylinder pressure than the spark plugs could handle. He turned the nitrous system off and flew the whole race without it. The extra weight of the fuel slowed him down. He finished the eight lap Gold race in fifth place at 407.565 mph. It was the first time in eleven years the Bearcat finished a Gold race at Reno.

Lyle congratulated all who were involved. "We wanted to win Reno, but the fact is we were fortunate to qualify and finish in the Gold after the failure of our new 'super-engine'. Our number one objective for 1987 is still to WIN RENO---and any other races that happen. Some interesting record attempts may be possible in the future. So, Dave has his program going to squeeze a good chunk of speed out of that fat little old airframe—at reduced power!"

Penney added his compliments. "Considering the task we were faced with and the time in which we were allowed to prepare *Rare Bear*, our finish can be seen as no less than an outstanding victory! CONGRATULATIONS!"

DeBoer also congratulated Lyle, Penney, Cornell and the crew for their performance. He could see the winning attitude from the group and was pleased to renew his sponsorship for the following year. Negotiations were conducted over the winter months as work progressed on the airplane. The hastily installed engine performed satisfactorily and served as a spare for several years.

Rick Brickert won the 1985 Reno race in Dreadnought at 434.488 mph.

Much attention had been focused on Sandberg's new Unlimited homebuilt. The Unlimited Division newsletter of September/October 1986 summarized *Tsunami*'s first race. "Between generator failures on Friday and Sunday, a broken auxiliary oil pump drive shaft on Saturday, and a lean ADI condition and backfire on Sunday, *Tsunami* did get a lot of beneficial test time and pylon experience to add to the previous three weeks of flight testing." They predicted *Tsunami* would be back to Reno in 1987 and ready to race.

The year ended with the Unlimited Division mourning the death of Bob Love on December 6, 1986. Love flew a P-51 in the first Reno Air Race held in 1964 and almost every one after that. He raced at Mojave, Lincoln, and San Diego; he also served as check pilot for rookies in the Unlimited Division. An Air Ace during the Korean conflict, a corporate pilot, a knowledgeable, interesting speaker, when Love talked about flying everyone paid close attention, usually learning something new.

Love's memorial services, held at Livermore Airport in California, attracted an assortment of P-51s, Stearmans, T-6s, T-28s, Skip Holm in *The Healer*, Lyle, John Crocker, and about 400 pilots, crews, friends, family, and admirers. An Air Force color guard marched in formation, stood for a moment of silence, then as the honor guard fired in salute the color guard folded the American flag for presentation to Love's son. Air racers Jack Hovey, Lloyd Hamilton, Dan Martin and San Francisco 49ers football player Russ Francis flew low over the nearby runway with Francis in his Sea Fury pulling away for the Missing Man formation. Those on the ground silently said their own farewell to a beloved friend.

After Love's memorial services Lyle visited the hangar of Bill Montagne, owner/builder of *Mach Buster*, a new pusher prop Unlimited air racer under construction. The skeleton of the aircraft sat on jacks; a sleek model of the airplane rested on a nearby table. A mechanic working on the plane answered questions as Lyle thoroughly inspected it. The plane had a body like a jet, engine based on a dragster, a pusher prop similar to the one being tested by General Electric for airliners, and a unique double articulating landing gear. The builder predicted it would reach speeds in excess of 600 mph.

"It might work," was Lyle's restrained comment.

Twelve years later the *Mach Buster* was sold to Bob Rose and was on exhibit in the pits in Reno. It had no engine and had never been tested or flown.

With DeBoer's renewed financial backing in 1987 Lyle was able to rent a hangar at the Van Nuys airport, hire Dave Cornell as full-time crew chief, and have *Rare Bear* completely overhauled. The engine was removed; all paint and bondo were stripped from the exterior; hydraulics, electrical systems and gear assembly were checked. For months the gutted airframe stood naked in the Van Nuys hangar while crew members attended to individual areas, restoring everything restorable.

Cornell found the plane fought them every step of the way. Nothing came easy. Parts that fit were not to be found, they had to be hand made. Screws had to be re-threaded, cowling pieces were individually formed. Phone calls to retired Curtiss Wright engineer Charlie Thompson, whom Lyle had contacted in 1969, again yielded valuable advice on modifying the engine. Cornell visited libraries to look up results of tests conducted over the years, researching information that could make the difference in another mile of two of speed. He was trying to improve the horsepower and further streamline the fuselage like the racers of the 1930s had done. In this he had help from aerodynamicists Carl Friend, Jim Chase, and Richard Tracy.

The urge to improve the performance of every aircraft he worked on drove Carl Friend to spend long hours, with slide rule in hand, going over every inch of *Rare Bear*. He was born in Columbus, Ohio but moved with his family to Southern California when he was seven years old at a time when airplane designs were changing rapidly. During WW II he worked for Lockheed Aircraft in Burbank, California. He helped develop notable planes like the P2V Neptune, P-38, XP-58, Constellation...and many more. After the war he worked at various times at Northrop, Bendix, Ryan, and again at Lockheed. While at Ryan he was a consultant on Lindberg's *Spirit of St. Louis*. His artist wife, Jane, has the walls of their Burbank home lined with commendations, certificates and pictures following her husband's illustrious career. Now Carl, seldom seen without his slide rule in hand, was dedicated to the Bearcat.

There was a problem with the latest engine...it had what was called a 'fast nose case'. The prop was spinning much faster compared to what it would do with the earlier engines. It restricted the amount of horsepower they could use and could result in a runaway prop. Even after the nose case was replaced by a Connie nose case Lyle consulted with Friend about changing to a different propeller. Carl discussed the possibilities with several other engineers---and with Lyle---before serious changes would be made.

Lockheed thermodynamicist Pete Law, who worked at Lockheed's famed super-secret 'Skunk Works', consulted with Cornell about improvements to the water regulator and carburetor. Together they installed splitter vanes in the inlet duct. Law a handsome man never without a smile or a twinkle in his eyes, kept the crew entertained with the stories he *couldn't* tell them about working at the Skunk Works.

When someone thought they had figured out what was going on over there, Law deadpanned, "I'd love to tell you all about it. But then, you know, I'd have to kill you!"

Greg Shaw helped install a special fuels system. Bill Prewitt reworked and refitted the cowling, a major undertaking. The list goes on and on.

All this activity did not go unnoticed in the racing fraternity. To questions asked Cornell replied, "Test flying has been done. We gathered some interesting data. Work is progressing satisfactorily. At this point I would rather not discuss what work is now in progress. That would spoil the surprise."

When the surprise was revealed later on it was a big one! But it was two years down the line.

Slowly the aircraft came back together. The crew worked feverishly nights and weekends. Several days had to be set aside to leave *Rare Bear* in the paint shop to re-apply the same paint scheme as last year. There was a new logo on the side – Wichita Air Services – one of DeBoer's companies. Time was running out when finally, on August 24, *Rare Bear* lifted off from Van Nuys Airport with Lyle at the controls for a successful test flight lasting about one hour.

Cornell praised the crew. "It was a group effort. Their hard work paid off in a speed increase of approximately 12 mph."

Ripples of excitement spread through the Reno Air Race pits in September, 1987, when Bill Destefani set a new qualifying record in his P-51 *Strega* of 466.674 mph. Then Hinton qualified *Tsunami* at 464.649 mph, faster than *Rare Bear's* qualifying speed of 452.490 mph. Everyone anticipated one of the fastest races on record – if the good weather held.

It was not the weather that dampened their hopes. When *Tsunami* experienced engine problems during lap 6 of a Saturday heat race, Hinton was forced to land. He touched down safely but as the plane was rolling out the right landing gear collapsed. The fuselage hit the ground, bent the prop blades, crunched the right wing tip, and broke a couple castings on the right gear. There was too much damage to repair overnight. The plane was first trucked to Chino to repair the wing and then trucked to Minneapolis for further repairs over the winter months.

Tsunami was out; now it was down to *Strega* and *Rare Bear*. The Bearcat crew quietly struggled to solve a coil problem that showed up Friday causing the engine to run very rough. Lyle elected to take off for the Gold race on Sunday and try different fuel settings to see if he could smooth is out. He could not so rather than blow the new engine he pulled out on the second lap. Destefani cruised the eight laps to finish first with a new race record of 452.559 mph. It would have been a story book ending for DeBoer and Lyle had *Rare Bear* breezed to first place in the Gold race. There was disappointment when it did not but the crew was more optimistic than at anytime in the past seven years.

DeBoer was a patient sponsor. He understood the enormous problems involved modifying and maintaining the *Rare Bear's* engine. There were no manuals to consult, many parts were hand-made, one-of-a –kind. He could often be seen with Lyle looking under the cowling, discussing the changes they saw.

He did more than provide funds for restoring the airplane and hiring a crew chief. He purchased a 48-foot drop frame trailer with side doors and a back lift gate for use by the crew. During the summer while some crew members were working on the airplane others were remodeling the inside of the trailer to provide a rest area at one end complete with refrigerator, microwave, coffee station, couch and table. The remaining area was outfitted as a workshop with workbenches, shelves and cupboards to store tools and spare parts. The outside of the trailer was painted in DeBoer's corporate colors to match the airplane. Crew members were proud to show off their new quarters when Lyle's mother and his aunt Irene (Ledbetter) arrived during the week to watch Lyle race.

DeBoer invited several employees and friends (Ski Bums of America) to the races. They were royally treated to a cocktail party Thursday night (crew members included) and a BBQ Saturday night held in a 30-foot by 30-foot tent erected next to the former Lear hangar at the west end of the field. During the day DeBoer's guests rested and had a catered lunch between races at a 33-foot RV located across the ramp from the Bearcat pit.

Crew members were smiling all week. "I can get used to this really quick," one happy mechanic proclaimed.

With all the speed records set by the Bearcat you would think it would fly from frigid Reno to balmy Van Nuys at close to Mach 1 after the races. No such luck. It took three months – most of it on the ground – to get from Reno to Mather Air Force Base near Sacramento.

Rare Bear had stayed at Stead until some of the crew came back in November to install a repaired carburetor. During shipping a careless baggage handler dropped the box containing the carburetor damaging the drive shaft. The trip was wasted. They came back in December to finish the repairs so Lyle could fly back to Van Nuys. When they arrived the temperatures were in the fifteen to twenty-five degree range; the engine was just as cold when they tried to start it; the fuel pump had to be replaced.

Unable to complete the work that weekend and needing another part they left the frozen city of Reno without the *Bear*. They returned on December 27th, completed the job, and were successful in getting the engine running. *Rare Bear* took off, destination Van Nuys.

Usually Lyle's VFR course followed Interstate 80 west out of Reno towards Sacramento. He was over Auburn, California (about forty miles northeast of Sacramento) when the engine began shuddering and the cylinder temperature dropped. He tried different fuel mixtures with no change in engine performance so he decided the prudent course was to set down at the nearest friendly field and check out the situation. Mather Air Force base was in sight. He radioed for permission to make an emergency landing, which they granted. He was met by an assortment of emergency and base security vehicles. He identified himself as a retired military pilot and explained the emergency. Then the 'Follow Me' truck led him to a remote area of the field where the base commander had driven out to meet him. It is not often the personnel on a SAC (Strategic Air Command) base get the opportunity to see a WW II Grumman F8F-2 Navy fighter airplane up close. The base commander and other personnel were very interested in looking it over.

The Air Force personnel were very hospitable and offered every assistance possible. They agreed to let the Bear stay there and let the crew have access to the field to work on the plane as soon as it was convenient for them. Some of the *Rare Bear* crew drove up to Mather on January 4th. This time they discovered a burnt coil, which meant another trip to Van Nuys for parts and another trip to Mather.

On January 15, Gregoire, Noctor, Wood and Cornell again drove to Mather. Lyle flew in to Sacramento, but once again he could not fly the Bear out. The crew completed the repairs to the engine and had it running smoothly. The problem this time was bad weather. Everyone returned to Van Nuys to wait for VFR conditions.

FINALLY! On Tuesday, January 19, Cornell and Lyle returned to Mather to retrieve the plane. Lyle flew it over to Sacramento Metro to refuel, then took off. Cornell followed on a commercial flight.

Cornell told the crew, "Now the countdown to Reno '88 can really begin."

16

Back in the Winner's Circle

Residents of northern California had long memories so when the idea of holding an air show or air race was brought up the specter of the F-86 exploding in flames at an ice cream parlor near Sacramento usually drowned any attempt to convince the public such an event could be safe or a benefit to their community. Nevertheless, in late 1987 an announcement was made that the United States Army had granted permission to the Hamilton Field Associates to use Hamilton Air Base in May for an air show and Unlimited air race. It was at Hamilton in 1964 that Lyle had missed his flight to Hawaii; he flew instead to Reno to see its first air race. So many changes had occurred in his life since that weekend. He looked forward to racing there.

.Many military aviators remembered the former Army Air Corps base that hangared P-40s, P-38s, P-51s, and some B-25s – to name a few – over forty-five years earlier. Located north of San Francisco, across the Golden Gate bridge, it was known as Marin Meadows Airfield when built in 1929. It was re-named Hamilton Field in 1932 after WW I air ace Lt. Lloyd Hamilton. The fabled B-17s took off from Hamilton for Hickam Field, Hawaii, arriving there on December 7, 1941, in the midst of the bombing of Pearl Harbor. Now F-101s and F-104s were based there until the installation would be deactivated in the near future.

The challenge to the Unlimited Division was to hold an absolutely safe, trouble-free race here in the middle of the highly populated area.

It was Wednesday before Mother's Day weekend when the planes and crews arrived at Hamilton Field to settle in and qualify. They were dismayed to find no defined pit spaces, no insurance provided by the promoters, no designated qualifying periods, and terrible weather. The day was darkly overcast, cold, showery, and very windy. The designated pit area had huge puddles where airplanes and support vehicles were meant to be parked. The images of parked planes reflected in mini-ponds provided photographers with some interesting pictures. Crews got wet feet. Tethered orange balloons were intended as pylons but high winds blew some of them loose from their moorings. Someone reported sighting one of the pylon balloons near Alameda, about twenty miles east across San Francisco Bay.

His TWA flight schedule had Lyle returning to Van Nuys Tuesday, May 3. He wanted to get at least one good night's sleep before starting the Hamilton Air Race activities. Qualifying was scheduled to begin Thursday on the 9.09 mile course; he planned his departure from Van Nuys that morning for the relatively short trip to Hamilton. Eighteen Unlimiteds were entered. *Rare Bear's* crew was already at Hamilton so he could qualify that same day, depending on weather. Cornell had reported to him that it was a tight course with four of its six pylons out over the water.

When *Rare Bear* touched down at Hamilton on Thursday nothing was happening. Only the plywood Home Pylon, positioned near the south end of the runway, was still standing. Threatened by insufficient insurance coverage and no defined race course, the pilots united their efforts to try to salvage this air race. By Friday they had obtained insurance, new pylons were set out and the pilots went on the honor system while qualifying. Pylon judges were unable to row out to their stations under the balloons because of choppy water and high winds.

A potentially life-threatening situation arose when unscheduled aircraft entered the traffic pattern during qualifying. The intruding pilots had not read, nor heeded, the NOTAMS (Notice to Airmen) which announced that Hamilton Field was closed to general aviation and military traffic during the air show/air race event. Quick responses by at least two Unlimited pilots prevented mid-air collisions.

Despite the unexpected distractions and intermittent showers most planes qualified on Saturday, led by *Rare Bear* at 411.095 mph. It was suspected that some of the pylons had drifted out of position so no one was certain if the course still measured 9.091 miles. This would affect the actual speeds registered but as everyone was flying the same course, it was accepted as official.

On Sunday the pylon judges braved the rough sea as they rowed out to their pylon stations in small boats and tried not to get blown away with the errant balloons. (They were dubbed "The NAG Navy" as most were officials trained and provided by the National Air-racing Group). The Unlimiteds were divided evenly to run in two races; their positions were determined by qualifying speeds. *Rare Bear* was racing in the Gold.

At the start of the Gold race Lyle jumped out in front of Destefani, last year's Reno champion, losing the lead only briefly on lap 1. He quickly regained the lead, then went on to win the Gold race at a speed of 412.487 mph. Destefani was only one and one-half seconds behind to finish at 412.284 mph. It was a close, exciting race. The jubilant *Rare Bear* crew's shouts of "THE BEAR IS BACK!" echoed the length of the ramp. The cream/copper frost/blue Bearcat with its new 'Warbirds Unlimited' logo (another of DeBoer's companies) on the sides looked good standing in the winner's circle in front of the grandstands. The crew proudly posed for pictures wearing their new black air race jackets. A smiling Lyle patiently posed in front of *Rare Bear* holding the silver trophy and signing dozens of autographs. It wasn't the biggest race of the year, yet it was probably the most satisfying.

Missing in the victory circle was sponsor DeBoer. It was reported he was hunting alligators from a dugout canoe on the Amazon River. The endless work of the crew that summer included: a new spinner from a Beverly Blackburn; behind the spinner is the afterbody that really smooths out the airflow to the cylinders—that took the most work. There was a lot of little stuff– engine cooling reduction; oil cooling reduction; reduced drag around the engine, new stack system.

"Today, on the rear cylinders, I finally had some temperatures that got up there – for a lot of years they have been running too cold. And we still have some other things to improve before Reno," Lyle explained.

Destefani commented, "It was an exciting race. I was with the Bearcat all the time, and Lyle flew a heck of a race. It was easy flying on his wing, that's what I was doing the whole time. And as we closed in on the final laps, he was whippin' his a little more and I was whippin' mine a little more. But I did not have the response I did at Reno and just did not get him. That's all there was to it. He flat out beat us! That little Bearcat ran good. Our airplane ran good, too—purred like a kitten and didn't come in with oil all over it. We can't ask for any more."

Rare Bear returned to Van Nuys and *Strega* returned to Bakersfield while each crew took a day or two off before beginning to fine tune their machines for a rematch in the high desert at Reno in September.

A widely publicized announcement in August heralded a new air racer to be built from scratch near Minneapolis, Minnesota. Bob Pond, a warbird collector, had commissioned Bert Rutan to design a totally new machine capable of challenging all existing speed records for piston engine propeller driven airplanes. It immediately became known as *the Pond Racer.*

In April, after the Hamilton race, Bonnie and Dave Cornell drove to Phoenix (115 degrees in a truck with no air conditioning), to bring back a DC-7 cowling to be modified and fitted onto the front of *Rare Bear.* It needed a lot of work, including filling in some bullet holes! Someone at sometime had apparently used this cowling for target practice. Prewitt did extensive sheet metal work modifying it to fit the Bear. He also stiffened the flame panels and belly, modified the hell-hole access door, and constructed a new spinner for the prop. Tom Graham flew in from DeBoer's aviation service in Wichita to help applying bondo, improving gap seals on elevators and ailerons, and smoothing in other rough spots. Photos taken by photographer Neal Nurmi of the Bearcat in flight showed the canopy was lifting about one-quarter inch so new fasteners were devised to correct the problem.

While the crew was busy modifying *Rare Bear* Lyle was in St. Louis for TWA's simulator training. He was back in Van Nuys in time to ferry *Rare Bear* to Reno on September 10.

When Lyle returned to air racing in 1980 it was his belief in himself and his airplane that inspired an inexperienced, volunteer crew to put their time and energy to work for him. Bill Jones and George Byard at Aircraft Cylinder Co. were generous with their donated parts. Mel

Gregoire's experience with the R-3350 engine was crucial. However, the team's appearance at the races from 1980 through 1987 was not a threat to the rest of the Unlimited field.

The *Rare Bear Air Racing Team* that showed up for the 1988 Reno Championship Air Races surprised a lot of their competition and a lot of loyal fans. *Rare Bear* retained the corporate colors of Jack DeBoer's company. The crew proudly wore their shiny, new embroidered black team jackets. After watching the hard-working crew emerge every day with oil stained clothes,the practical sponsor chose black jackets rather than using his much lighter corporate colors. The 48 foot team trailer shared the pit space with *Rare Bear* wearing matching logos and colors. It was the new attitude that was so obvious to all....Confidence! Pilot, crew and sponsor stood tall in the pits. Their win at Hamilton against the number one competitor in the Unlimited field validated their hard work and belief they 'can do.' Lyle was the center of attention wherever he went. There were a lot of smiles in the *Rare Bear* pit this year.

In the Pits, 1989.
Neal Nurmi

When Lyle went out on the new 9.171 mile Unlimited course to qualify on Monday there were sunny skies, temperatures in the 60s, gusty winds and the air hazy from nearby brush fires. He wasted no time letting the competition know he was racing for the Gold as he qualified at a record breaking 474.622 mph. Destefani, who set a record one year ago, had engine problems that forced him to land without qualifying. Repairs could not be made so the much anticipated rematch between *Rare Bear* and *Strega* was postponed until next year.

The *Rare Bear* crew was impressed with their new sponsor when he and his guests touched down at Stead Field in a Gulfstream Four and a Lear Jet 35. DeBoer came with gifts for the crew---black, embroidered and personalized tote bags to match their team jackets---which he presented to them at a party he hosted at the hotel in the evening. Lyle and Cornell thanked DeBoer and gave a pep talk to the crew about the upcoming Championship race on Sunday. This was not your usual air race week for them.

The Unlimiteds in Friday's Heat 2A race were not pushing their racers to the limit. *Rare Bear* crossed the finish line first at a modest speed of 423.401 mph. Saturday's heat race was memorable and came to be known as the "mayday" race. Don Whittington in *Precious Metal* declared a mayday on lap 3, then landed safely. On lap 4, Scott Sherman in *Stilleto*, John Maloney in *Super Corsair*, and Lyle in *Rare Bear* declared maydays within moments of one another. Sherman and Maloney landed safely while Lyle was on final approach. Before Lyle touched down Jimmy Leeward in *Leeward Air Ranch Special* declared a mayday. With Lyle still landing on one runway Leeward lined up for runway 35 only to find a fuel truck parked in the middle. He quickly spotted a little dirt road where he bellied in. Then, as he tried to slow down, he was stunned to see two helicopters plus some people sitting in lawn chairs dead ahead. He braked hard as he tried to swing ninety degrees left. As the plane spun around over the rough terrain his prop tips grazed the ground. When the dust settled Leeward was unhurt but his recently restored airplane had multiple injuries including damaged prop tips.

Steve Hinton in *Tsunami* survived to win and establish a new six-lap record of 462.218 mph. Only two other planes of the original seven finished the race and landed safely: Rick Brickert in *Dreadnought* and Lloyd Hamilton in *Furias*.

Lyle said, "I had to mayday when air rushing through a gear door gap back pressured the left hot exhaust vent outward funneling smoke and fumes into the cockpit. I dropped down real quick."

After the plane was towed into the pits the crew assured everyone they could repair the damage and they would have #77 in the Gold race on Sunday. The Beacat pit was the center of attention later when the airplane was raised up on jacks. Cornell lost no time in having retraction tests and adjustments made to the pocket doors on the landing gear.

The vendor's stands around the grandstands had been crowded all day. Sunday afternoon, when Bob Hoover assembled the Unlimited pilots in a lineup in front of their planes on the ramp in front of the grandstands, spectators hurried back to their seats. Nobody wanted to miss the Gold race.

Hoover repeated his safety procedures, as he had for so many years, to the pilots ready to take off, fly fifty feet above the ground at speeds approaching 500 mph, close to each other, around pylons beckoning them to make tight turns.

As the pilots climbed into their cockpits and readied for take off, crews and spectators found their favorite observations spots. The top of the *Rare Bear* support trailer was lined with people. Fans on the flight line stood shoulder-to-shoulder, ready to scream their support for their team.

The Rare Bear crew, some standing in the back of a pickup truck, were happy and anxious. They were hoping this was the day #77 would make it back to the winner's circle at Reno.

As he flew each lap in the low, precise groove that is Lyle's style there was growing excitement at the prospect of his first Reno win in twelve years. When he flashed past the start/finish pylon with a new eight-lap race record of 456.821 mph the crew and the crowd erupted with cheers and tears of joy. The 1988 *Rare Bear* finished 35.131 mph faster than its 1975 Gold race winning speed! It was impossible for the delirious crew to put into words their emotions as they sped across the ramp to join their plane and their pilot in front of the grandstands as champions!

The supremely happy pilot commented, 'My crew prepared the airplane, and it was all set to go. They are the best crew in the world—they made it all possible. I got out in front where I could fly my own course without any prop wash, without having to get away from anybody. That is the only way to fly a race, believe me. I was very comfortable up front, relatively speaking, other than getting the hell beat out of me in an extremely hostile cockpit environment. However, at the power I was using, it was as smooth a running R-3350 engine I have ever sat behind. For a 3350 that's not too smooth, but it was as smooth as any of these round bangers ever are.'

At the annual air race dinner that evening a beaming Lyle accepted his first place trophy and check while the crew, Jack DeBoer, and many supporters joined him on stage. One of the race sponsors, Air Camel, also awarded him with a $10,000 check (written on a 3' x 5' foam core board), for his championship win.

17

SMASHING THE 500 MPH BARRIER

Traditionally, the speaker at the annual NAG banquet, held in Oakland, California, is the previous year's Gold race winner from one of the four air race divisions. In January, 1989---as 1988 Unlimited winner---Lyle gave the crowd an entertaining talk covering his many years rounding the pylons in *Rare Bear*, maydays, and disappointments. Photographer Neal Nurmi provided slides from his extensive collection that prompted memories for the many air race fans. By evening's end Lyle had doffed his jacket and tie, answered dozens of questions. Everyone reluctantly left the restaurant when the manager said it was 'closing time'.

Later in January, Lyle made a 'top-secret' visit to photographer Bucky Dawson in Ketchikan, Alaska. Dawson told those who asked about the visit that Lyle was there to check progress on his top-secret

Seaplane project "Big Red Mama", an R-4360-modified DHC-3 Otter. Dawson said he and his crew were working at a furious pace to ready the plane for an assault upon the World Seaplane Propeller speed record after trying for the landplane record with *Rare Bear*. There were more hints about the project: radical airframe and system mods, mating a new secret custom-designed composite wing and tail. At this point in their story, Dawson and Lyle were observed winking broadly at each other.

"We wouldn't say all this if it wasn't true, would we?", they smiled.

The "top secret" project remains secret to this day.

It had been many years since Lyle had a real vacation that didn't relate to *Rare Bear*. He vowed to return soon to Alaska for some serious salmon and halibut fishing.

When *Rare Bear* sat in the pits during air races the mechanics always found something needed to be done---bolts to be tightened, wiring to be checked, screens to be pulled and examined for anything suspicious. Fans gathered behind the ropes surrounding the pit watching, wondering, often commenting, "round engines leak oil…a lot of oil." Others nodded in agreement. Each day, when the plane came back from flying, volunteers were ready to clean oil off the sides and belly, polish again the area they had polished an hour or two earlier, sit back and wait until the next flight was over. Then they could do it again. Over the years the team had experimented with numerous cleaners and polishing compounds, from car wax to cornstarch. Volunteers worked hard to make the air flow smoothly over the wings and down the sides. It might add another mile of speed and win the race. Aerodynamicists had recommended sealing gaps and smoothing surfaces to improve the air flow. The goal was always more speed.

There was another way to improve their speed – more horsepower. For twenty years Lyle had found the Wright R-3350 engine, with various modifications, was up to the task of producing increasingly greater horsepower. He had tried various propeller/spinner combinations, always four blades, with varying degrees of efficiency. While the complete overhaul of the airplane was underway in 1987 there was neither the time nor the money to experiment with a new propeller. When the *Bear* returned to Van Nuys following the long winter it spent at Stead in 1987 the crew had little time to do anything but routine maintenance before the Hamilton race. That didn't mean they had forgotten the propeller project. Winning two races in 1988 showed them they were on the right track with the engine – but so were several competitors. A more efficient propeller was needed.

Carl Friend and Lyle decided to try a broader blade to see if it would overcome the problems *Rare Bear* was currently encountering with prop blade tip speeds. The search for a suitable blade resulted in modifying a P-3 Orion four-blade propeller to a three-blade propeller. The intent was to go with three blades but blades with a lifting surface adequate to convert horsepower to thrust.

Lyle explained, "Carl came up with the proposal that these broader blades modified to three blades could convert as much horsepower-to-thrust as four blades but do it more efficiently. First of all, there is better aerodynamics on the blade. Those P-3 blades are a lot slicker and thinner."

The installation and testing of the modified blades was conducted at the beginning of summer. They found some handling problems that required more engineering and adjustments so the propeller was removed and replaced by the old four-blade propeller. The massive R-3350 engine and huge three-blade propeller out front changed the directional trim . That changed the handling for the pilot too much; the project was postponed until after the 3-Km speed record challenge scheduled in August and the Reno races that followed a few weeks later. A lot of work to be done – not much time to do it.

It's hard to break a world record. Before the 1976 incident in Mojave that ended with the Bear's seized engine and bent propeller blades Lyle had announced his intention to try to break the 3-Km speed record for piston engine aircraft. Darryl Greenamyer held the record until August, 1979 when Steve Hinton established the new record of 499.018 mph. The 500 mph barrier was still there. The 500 mph barrier was the one Lyle wanted to break.

The *Rare Bear* was in peak condition, even without the new propeller. Lyle contacted the NAA (National Aeronautics Association) to reserve the months of June, July and August to make his attempt. He and his long-time TWA friend, Ray Lutz, scouted several airports, checked summer weather conditions for each of them, then chose the historic, picturesque old town of Las Vegas, New Mexico, for the attempt. Once it was a main stop on the Santa Fe Trail; now the 17,000 residents lived quietly while tourists flocked to the nearby cities of Santa Fe, Albuquerque and Taos. The airport chosen for the speed run was located three miles outside of town, elevation 6,874 feet. Lyle encouraged Jack DeBoer to join him and set a speed record in his new Lear 31 jet, as no record currently existed for that class. Ray Cote of the International Formula One class was also invited to join the venture to challenge the old Formula One record.

Before a speed run can be attempted many logistical and administrative tasks are required. Tom Gribben of Pyramid Engineering in Reno, Nevada flew to the site to plan and survey the proposed course. Wanda Odom of the NAA in Washington, DC and Earl Hanson of the NAA in Los Angeles guided the pilots through the necessary applications and paperwork. Dick Freeborg of Instrumentation Marketing in Burbank, California agreed to bring his high tech cameras and timing equipment to the site. FAA officials reviewed regulations governing air traffic in and around the area during the run itself.

Las Vegas hotels and motels were booked. The Las Vegas Chamber of Commerce threw their support behind the project by making available a hangar at the airfield and contacting local media to ensure good coverage for the event

A farmer who owned the pasture next to the airport gave permission to have the equipment set up on his land. The day before the scheduled arrival of the pilots and planes, Gribben, with help from *Rare Bear* crew member Hersch Rourk and Unlimited Division secretary-treasurer Jack Sweeney, began surveying and marking the three kilometer course with plastic panels on the ground. When they went back to the field the next day to check the arrangements the panels were gone---they had been eaten by some of the cattle. New panels were laid out and protected by hastily erected barbed wire enclosures. Freeborg arrived and sited camera stations in accordance with standards set by the NAA.

A three-kilometer speed run course measures a total of five kilometers with speed timed over the center three kilometers. The pilot cannot go above 150 meters above the reference ground elevation on the course, or above 500 meters on the turn arounds. In a thirty-minute period the pilot can make unlimited passes over the course; the record is based on the four fastest consecutive passes. Ground spotters are located at each end of the five-kilometer markers. Sophisticated cameras capable of shooting 200 frames per second are located at each end of the 3-km course. Three spotter aircraft are in the air, one at each end and one close to the middle of the course, to verify the aircraft does not exceed the allowable altitude during the speed run. All records are considered unofficial until the NAA has reviewed the video film and recalculated the speeds. These records are then sent to the FAI (Federation Aeronautique Internationale) in Paris, France, for certification of the world record.

The small town of Las Vegas was overwhelmed by engineers, NAA and FAA officials, surveyors, timers, camera operators, crew members, family and friends – all to watch three pilots and three airplanes fly back and forth, one at a time, over a 5-Km course. One morning on their way to the airfield several crew members watched as a black bear climbed a tree in a resident's yard. It was assumed the black bear in the tree wanted to watch the *Rare Bear* in the air.

A problem popped up in the *Bear's* ignition system and there was a minor oil leak which Crew Chief Gordon Symon wanted to fix before the plane left Van Nuys for New Mexico. The repairs took a few days longer than anticipated so Lyle did not actually arrive at the speed run site until Friday. DeBoer and Cote were already there and planning their flights.

DeBoer, piloting his new Lear 31 jet with Craig Tylski of the Learjet Corporation as co-pilot, established the first light jet 3-Km speed record at 480.223 mph on Saturday, August 19, 1989. On Sunday, August 20, Ray Cote of El Cajon, California, with his wife Gladys as crew, attempted to break the 261 mph record for the Formula One class in his air racer *Alley Cat*. On his third pass he threw a rod in the engine. He was able to make a successful landing but could not repair the engine on site and had to abandon the attempt.

After Cote's flight Lyle made his first try for the record. It ended when his cooling system developed a leak. After landing he was towed to the hangar where the crew worked quickly to repair the system. Shortly after noon Lyle took off again. After making the required four consecutive passes the results were calculated and showed he had unofficially established a new record of 515.766 mph. Everyone was delighted; the 500 mph barrier was gone!

"Not good enough," said Lyle.

He asked crew members, timers and various officials to stay over one more day to give him a chance to break his own record.

On Monday morning he again experienced problems in the carburetor air induction system. He had completed three passes, one timed at 541 mph, before he had to pull off the course. Time was running out. The crew worked frantically to make the adjustments. The NAA and FAA officials had to leave that afternoon. The wind was picking up and the temperature dropped a few degrees when *Rare Bear* went back onto the

New Speed Record, 528.33 mph
Somers Blackman

course.

At 3:30 p.m. on August 21, 1989, Lyle established the new 3-Km speed record for piston engine propeller driven airplanes at 528.329 mph (850.24 kph). This was 29.11 mph above Hinton's 1979 speed!.

Lyle thanked DeBoer for his generous financial help. DeBoer spent well over $20,000 to cover the expenses needed to get the two new speed records into the books. Without his sponsorship this record would not have been set.

Lyle was quick to praise *Rare Bear* crew members and supporters for their extraordinary efforts. Steve Murphy, FBO Manager at the Las Vegas Municipal Airport, his wife Susan, and their two children were thanked for their hospitality and many, many errands they had performed. Lyle included Jerry Van Citters, long-time Reno and Mojave pylon judge, who had come from Los Angeles via Amtrak to serve as a volunteer observer. Former Bearcat crew member Bill Coulter, now living in Santa Fe, had driven up to volunteer his help. He quickly found himself transporting dry ice and other supplies from Santa Fe and now heard Lyle express his appreciation.

Lyle's mother, Ida Mae Shelton, had driven with her grandson and a nephew, Jerome Head, from their home in Brownfield, Texas to provide moral support. They were proud spectators as they watched the little boy who loved airplanes achieve his long-held dream in the airplane he had rescued from a dusty weed patch in Indiana. He was flying fast!

A poem written by David M. Ward of Espanola, New Mexico, captured some of the emotion of the event:

A MAN AND A BEAR

Soft winds blow across grass-covered hills.
An eagle spirals up an invisible staircase.
White clouds dot a bowl of azure and march
In formation across the hemisphere of the sky.
Suddenly a distant thunder sweeps the earth
As a small speck on the horizon swiftly takes shape.
The object sprouts wings as it comes ever nearer
And becomes a hurtling airplane roaring into glory.
Eighty six years stretch out behind the aircraft
From the plains of New Mexico to the dunes of North Carolina
Years of triumphs and tragedies but none more memorable
Than this day of new heights of achievement for man and machine.
A Rare Bear and a rare man in command.
A symphony of power and speed and delicate control.
Old standards tumble as never before in the history of flight.
To the craft belongs the power. To the man belongs the glory.
Not for this man the puny increments of former successes.
A half century is compressed into one glorious day.
A Rare Bear has shattered other's dreams of domination
And a rare man has set a mark for future generations.

DAVID M. WARD, AUGUST, 1989

Glen Curtiss set the first airplane speed record of 47.65 mph in August, 1909. Lyle Shelton set the new speed record of 528.329 mph in August, 1989. Eighty years of old records tumbling and new records set that will tempt another pilot another day. Whether it be two youngsters racing their tricycles down a country road or Clay Lacy establishing a

Boeing 747-SP round-the-world speed record of 23,000 miles in 36 hours, 54 minutes, 15 seconds in January, 1988, records will be challenged by the men who hunger for speed.

Before the Reno races in September, 1989, John Sandberg mounted the first challenge to Lyle's new record. He took his custom built air racer *Tsunami* to Wendover, Utah. For the first three days the *Tsunami* crew was delayed by minor problems. Their impatience turned to despair on the fourth day when the left gear collapsed on a landing after a practice hop. A wing and the propeller were damaged ending their valiant efforts. They vowed to try again. And they promised they would have the broken airplane mended in time for the upcoming Reno Air Races.

The Unlimited entry list for the 1989 Reno races included nine former Gold Race champions:

1973, 1975 and 1988: Lyle Shelton in F8F Grumman Bearcat *Rare Bear*

1976: Lefty Gardner in P-51 *Thunderbird*

1978 and 1985: Steve Hinton in RB-51 *Red Baron* and F2G *Super Corsair*

1979: John Crocker in P-51 *Sumthin' Else*

1981 and 1984: Skip Holm in P-51 *Jeannie* and P-51 *Stiletto*

1982: Ron Hevle in P-51 *Dago Red*

1983: Neil Anderson in Sea Fury *Dreadnought*

1986: Rick Brickert in Sea Fury *Dreadnought*

1987: Bill Destefani in P-51 *Strega*

There was an upbeat mood throughout the pits on Monday as qualifying started in ideal weather. Everyone was ready and several pilots were dedicated to preventing *Rare Bear* from repeating its 1988 win. There was disappointment when *The Pond Racer* was not ready for this year's competition. Lyle was there to win again and showed it on Tuesday by qualifying at 467.378 mph. No one topped him so he started Friday's six-lap heat race in pole position.

The weather had cooled and winds had picked up. Dust devils, whirling tornado-like columns of sand rising from the desert floor, caused a fatal accident in the Formula One class that morning when one of the small racers disintegrated as it was engulfed by one of these ferocious little monsters. The bumpy air kept speeds down on Friday and Saturday, but Lyle managed to win both days.

On Sunday competition from the former gold race winners had thinned down to Rick Brickert in *Dreadnought*, Steve Hinton in *Tsunami*, John Crocker in *Sumthin' Else*, and Bill Destefani in *Strega*. The wind chill temperatures were in the freezing range; strong winds were blowing down from the northwest off Peavine mountain. The Sierra storm had dropped temperatures 35 degrees in two days. Lyle took his time coming off the pace lap. He had been penalized Friday and Saturday for cutting pylon 3. He didn't intend to do it a third time. The race turned into a duel between *Rare Bear* and *Strega* until lap 6 when Destefani pulled out with a broken coolant line. When Lyle's crew informed him that *Strega* was out and how many seconds he was ahead of the second place plane, he backed off the power. Both he and *Rare Bear* were taking a beating in the rough air. There was no need to punish themselves unnecessarily. His first place finish of 450.910 mph was anti-climatic with the number one competitor out of the race. Pilots, crews and spectators were expecting a photo finish. All were disappointed it did not happen.

The air race banquet held Sunday night after the races found the entire *Rare Bear* crew once again going on stage to receive the trophy, winner's check, and Air Camel's oversized check for $10,000. A few whispered that maybe next year they could "three-peat". *Rare Bear* stood silent in the hangar.

Lyle said, "We'll try".

The year ended with a crew party, held in Van Nuys, California, with about two-hundred crew members and *Rare Bear* supporters in attendance. The crew presented Lyle with a portable "moo marker" in case he attempted another speed record. The marker, which admittedly resembled the New Mexico cows that had grazed in the fields Lyle flew over during the speed run, can be positioned as a visual aid to the pilot. Lyle tried hard not to laugh as he thanked his crew for their thoughtful 'gift'.

Rare Bear had been carrying Lyle around pylons at air races over a twenty-one year span. They had established a new Time-to-Climb record, a new 3-Km speed record, and repeatedly broken qualifying and race records – some they had set. Yet Lyle still felt the need to fly faster. He was fifty-seven years old and looking for new ways to modify his aging partner, *Rare Bear*, so together they can fly faster. Their next modification would attract everyone's attention both on the ground and in the air.

18

THE GREAT BLADE

The National Air-racing Group again invited Lyle to speak at their annual banquet in January. TWA had Lyle scheduled to fly to Frankfort that weekend so Crew Chief Gordon Symon filled in for him.

"Lyle apologizes for not being here but plans to be here next year... unless that pesky little Italian gets in our way", declared Symon. Destefani, the "pesky little Italian," immediately announced HIS intentions of being next year's winner and speaker!

On March 12, 1990, the NAA, representing the Federation Aeronautique Internationale in the United States, presented Lyle with a plague in recognition of the new United States National Record, Class C-1, Piston Engine Propeller-driven Airplane Speed of 528.33 mph (850.24 kph) over a three-kilometer course at Las Vegas, New Mexico, he set on August 21, 1989. Jack DeBoer also received a plaque in recognition of his record set for the Lear Jet, Business Class, that same week. The ceremony, attended by about 300 people, was held in the Langley Auditorium of the Smithsonian National Air and Space Museum in Washington, D.C. Scott Crossfield, X-15 rocket pilot and the first man to fly faster than twice the speed of sound, presented the awards. Mel Gross served as Master of Ceremonies. Among other awards made that day was one to the Helicopter Club of America in recognition of their clean sweep of the World Championships in September, 1989.

Cal Poly students who built and flew the first human powered helicopter received a national certificate. The Lockheed Corporation received a certificate in recognition of the cross country speed record set by the SR-71 Blackbird. Overall about twenty-five awards were made.

Some of the recipients were able to tour the Paul E. Garber Preservation, Restoration and Storage Facility located at nearby Suitland, Maryland. The group watched work being done on the historic WW II B-29 bomber *Enola Gay*, which eventually will be on display at the Smithsonian's new facility at Dulles Airport. The tour guide asked Lyle to tell the group how he broke the old 3-Km speed record and a little bit about flying the Bearcat itself. Lyle explained the differences between Greenamyer's Bearcat *Conquest 1* and his own Bearcat. He also gave a brief history of how he located and restored the wreck to become the record setting *Rare Bear*.

When asked about his favorite aircraft at the Smithsonian, he replied, "Roscoe Turner's Laird-Turner *Meteor*, winner of the Thompson Trophy races at Cleveland in 1938 and 1939. The races were thirty laps – 300 miles total then. Imagine the fuel they had to carry!"

Air race fans were surprised to read in the March 30 edition of the Reno Gazette Journal a story by reporter Phil Barber headlined "*TOP GUNS OF RENO AIR RACES THREATEN BOYCOTT*" He reported that Bill Destefani, president of the pilot's group Air Racing Unlimited, claimed inadequate prize money and shabby treatment of pilots and crews at the race site as basis for the boycott. Negotiations were conducted during the spring. At the end of July the newspaper announced that prize money of $100,000 was guaranteed to the Unlimited air racers. Other concerns were addressed with a limited understanding being reached between the two sides. The races went on as scheduled with further discussions taking place after the end of the racing season.

Testing on the Bear's new three-blade prop resumed early in 1990. The project was complicated. What the engineers were proposing to do was daring and it was expensive. In the Volume 36, #2 Summer 1991 issue of the American Aviation Association Journal noted author Birch Matthews' article *RARE BEAR, A GOLD RACE RECORD AT RENO*, relates his discussions with Carl Friend about the deliberations and decisions leading to the selection of the radical new propeller.

Friend stated the new propeller obviously should have decreased thickness-to-chord blades and consequently lower blade section drag due to compressible airflow for greater efficiency. Improved efficiency would decrease power requirements at current speeds increasing engine life and help reliability. Furthermore, increased propulsive efficiency would provide a higher speed with ultimate engine power.

Matthews then quotes Carl Friend: "The only successful American high-speed, high-power propeller widely used is the four-blade Hamilton Standard (blade number 7121A-0) installed on the Lockheed Electra, Orion and Hercules aircraft. The latter uses a similar but not identical propeller blade. This design provides the required strength coupled with a low thickness-to-chord ratio. It is a solid blade made of forged aluminum alloy. However, increased blade chord and airfoil surface area with these propeller blades are accompanied by more aerodynamic drag and thus significantly decreased thrust with the Bearcat installation. This thrust loss was alleviated by reducing the total blade area simply by going down from four blades to three. Fortunately, a Lockheed 1649 *Star Constellation* 33E60 Hamilton Standard three-way engine-propeller hub is compatible with the new blades and R-3350 engine-propeller shaft used on the Bearcat."

By the middle of summer Lyle declared he was "moderately satisfied" with the results of tests on the new propeller. "The Bearcat has been tied down with heavy chains while the engine was run full throttle, testing the propeller for balance and harmonic flutter. Engine problems developed that we suspect are the result of the heavy strain put on it during the prop testing. We'll have to keep working on it until time to leave for Reno."

Rare Bear missed two Unlimited races during the summer months while the crew struggled with the new propeller blades. The Texas Air Races were held in June at Denison, Texas and the Denver Air Races in August at Front Range Airport, Colorado.

It was an unfamiliar feeling for Lyle to be at an air race without flying in it. He sat in the announcer's booth doing color commentary. It also gave him the chance to wander through the pits and watch the other crews in action, ask questions, and relax. He rarely had an opportunity to relax at an air race.

The Denver race is remembered as the first time a female pilot passed all the tests necessary to be allowed out on the course with the rest of the Unlimiteds in an actual race. Erin Rheinschild, wife of *Risky Business* pilot/owner Bill Rheinschild, became a qualified Unlimited air race pilot in her P-51 *No Business*. She placed sixth in her heat race on Saturday. She declared a mayday, then landed safely on Sunday.

Thirty-six unlimited planes entered the Reno races in September, 1990; twenty-one featured inline engines; fifteen were powered by radials.

The Great Blade
C. Aro

"Awesome! Unbelievable! Looks like three tongue depressors stuck to the nose." These were comments heard when *Rare Bear* arrived in the pits that week with its new propeller up front. Lyle and the crew were having fun responding to the reactions.

The most often heard comment, "I've never seen anything like it." Nobody was overly impressed by its performance after Lyle qualified second at 468.369 mph behind Destefani and *Strega*, who recorded 470.246 mph.

After the finish of the Friday heat race other pilots on the course said they knew when *Rare Bear* was close by. The big blades sent out vibrations that literally shook the planes behind it leaving a massive wake turbulence. Some said they could hear a sound they described as a distinct "whump, whump, whump."

Rookie pilot Robert Converse of *Huntress III* summed up his reaction to being passed by the Bear: "Wow, what a rush!"

Rare Bear wasn't alone in attracting attention now. As he walked around the pits wearing his colorful blue, orange, yellow and white flight suit, Lyle frequently was stopped for an autograph or by someone who asked questions about the airplane, the crew, the experience of flying so fast and so close to the ground. Some wanted to tell him about the first time they had watched him race. Sponsor DeBoer, grinning as Lyle answered questions, sometimes found himself the target of their curiosity. Occasionally Lyle had to excuse himself and hurry on to a pilot's briefing or to check on weather predicted for race time. Both men thoroughly enjoyed stopping to talk with the fans and listen to what thrilled them most.

It was not a surprise to them when many answered, "Speed. Watching the planes fly fast!"

Sunday's championship race was one of those tremendously exciting races you were glad you witnessed or sad you missed. Lyle, Skip Holm and Destefani each pushed their aircraft to the limit. Holm, in *Tsunami*, dashed out to an early lead as the planes came down the chute. Lyle gradually gained on him passing him by the third lap. From then on the radical new three-blade prop plus the powerful R-3350 engine propelled *Rare Bear* to the fastest speed thus far recorded for an Unlimited Gold race, 468.620 mph. This was the third consecutive win for the *Rare Bear Air Racing Team*. Members of the Unlimited Division rejoiced that it was a Gold race with no maydays.

Not satisfied with the overall performance of the new propeller co-crew chiefs Greg Shaw and Carl Schutte remarked their initial expectations were for a 15 mph speed increase. They declared there was more work to be done to bring it to maximum efficiency. That was fair warning to the other competitors that *Rare Bear* would be back next year.

Poet David Ward, author of the 1989 tribute to Lyle, saw the new propeller and was inspired to write another poem.

The Greate Blayde

The oracle sayeth "Possessed of a greater blayde
The Bear can, yea, slay its enemies",
And, forsooth, a blayde of wondrous breadth
Was given unto the Bear and it did become
Quite fearsome and a plague unto its foes
But soon did the master of the Bear
Become discontent and sayeth unto the oracle,
"The greate blayde is disquieting and brings distress
And unhappiness upon the Bear", but the oracle
Was adamant and the greate blayde remained.
Then it came to pass the foes of the Bear
Proclaimed fearsome passages were being rent
Into the firmament by the cleaving of the blayde
And terrible whirlwinds were borne of the passages
To toss their craft about with unseeming violence.
Soon did the Bear become master of all it surveyed
With the greate blayde he winged a pathway
To create a victorious trail, and thus
Did the master of the Bear become content
And proclaim to the oracle, It is well!"
And so endeth 1990

DAVID WARD, 1990

Sunday evening the National Championship Air Racing Association hosted the annual Awards Banquet. A large crowd listened as Lyle praised his crew for their countless hours of very hard work to get *Rare Bear* across the finish line first for the third time. He told a little of the efforts Carl Friend had made to get that impressive propeller modified to carry him to the increased speeds. The crew felt confident and ready for the challenge to win four in a row.

In November Jane and Carl Friend hosted a crew party at their home in Burbank. Crew members were used to seeing one another in grubby, oil-smeared work clothes, dark smudges on faces and hands. Tonight they wore casual shirts and clean slacks. There was not a trace of engine oil to be seen on this happy group. Lyle, smiling and looking relaxed appeared in his usual short-sleeve shirt, western style pants, and cowboy boots. Pictures showing Carl with some of the planes he had helped design were displayed throughout the house. Airplanes and speed dominated most conversations. Some were remembering past successes; some were speculating on future challenges.

19

FOUR IN A ROW

On February 28, 1991, Lyle Shelton retired from TWA after flying Boeing 727s, 707s, DC-9s, MD-80s and L-1011s for the past twenty-five years, both in the United States and Europe. One week after retiring he flew to Alaska for a week's visit with photographer Don "Bucky" Dawson. As the two friends flew over the spectacular, snowy Alaskan countryside Lyle couldn't help comparing the peaceful landscape beneath him to the crowded, frantic scenes as he flew over the Los Angeles area. This was a great place to relax.

After twenty-five years of irregular airline schedules Lyle wanted to have some thing to do that was both relaxing and challenging. He began helping long-time friend, Oscar Margraf, inspect his old gold mine near Tonopah, Nevada. Margraf wanted to explore the possibility of re-opening and developing the mine. There had been many changes in mining technology since Lyle's early college years so he enrolled in some mining and engineering courses at the University of Nevada-Reno. It was fun to be back on a college campus and in the classroom. He rented a small apartment in Reno and began splitting his time between Reno, the Tonopah area, and Granada Hills, California. *Rare Bear* was safely hangared in Van Nuys being tended by its faithful crew. Lyle was busier now than he had been as an airline captain and he was enjoying the change.

The *Pond Racer* made its long-awaited debut on April 4, 1991 at the Mojave Airport. Owner Bob Pond, a Minneapolis industrialist and former WW II pilot, invited Lyle to bring *Rare Bear* to Mojave for the media event billed as "The Champion and the Challenger." Pond intended to try to break Shelton's 3-Km speed record in August. Also present at the gathering were the *Pond Racer* designer, Burt Rutan, and his brother Dick. Burt Rutan was already noted for designing and building the aircraft *Voyager* which made aviation history as the first non-stop, un-refueled aircraft to fly around the world. *Rare Bear* and *Pond Racer* were photographed together but did not try to fly together.

Rutan made a short speech about the new racer, telling the assembly, "The airplane is designed to achieve speeds up to 528 mph. It easily reached 360 mph on its initial flight." The 528 mph figure just happened to be Lyle's speed when he established the new record almost two years earlier. Rutan, Pond, and Lyle spent a couple hours comparing ideas each one had about making fast airplanes fly faster. With his recent successes Lyle was comfortable with the Bearcat's capabilities; he was, of course, eager to listen to and evaluate new technology that might push his winning speed at Reno over the 500 mph barrier.

Qualifying at the 1991 Reno Air Races began on Monday, September ninth, under dreary skies. Rick Brickert qualified the *Pond Racer* at 400.10 mph. With improved weather on Tuesday Lyle went out and blistered the course with a new record-shattering qualifying speed of 475.899 mph. Qualifying was over and the engine was in good shape.

The *Rare Bear* pit was relaxed; even Lyle's chocolate labrador, B.J. visited and 'toured' the scene. A 'story board' was displayed at the edge of the pit, in front of the airplane, answering the most often questions for the spectators. Lyle was free to spend time in a vendor's tent signing autographs, posing for photos, and chatting with his fans. Crew members were looking for their fourth win in a row.

Qualifying continued through Wednesday. *Tsunami*, flown by Skip Holm, placed second at 456.908 mph. (Steve Hinton was recovering from injuries suffered when he crashed while filming a movie late in 1990) Nine other racers qualified over 400 mph, including Destefani in *Strega*.

Brickert did not declare an emergency as he came down the chute onto the race course on Thursday but he immediately pulled the airplane up and out of the heat race. The plane had a lot of oil covering one boom when it landed. Brickert insisted it was a minor problem; he would be racing on Friday. On Friday his problems continued and he again dropped out. He was able to coax the aircraft to a last place finish in the Silver heat on Saturday. At the beginning of the Sunday race the airplane began shaking and burning as the formation circled Peavine Mountain. Brickert used the on-board extinguisher to douse the fire. He landed safely with only one engine. Bob Pond promised testing would continue throughout the coming year and the *Pond Racer* would be in Reno in 1992.

Penney took *Rare Bear* onto the course for the Friday heat race. He said, "My mission, as spare pilot, is to fly the airplane at the manifold pressure, rpm and power settings assigned by Crew Chief Greg Shaw. It is not cool for the spare pilot to go out and break the engine so the pilot cannot go out and race. The crew is always looking for performance numbers so I collect data for them and they use it to make adjustments."

He admitted it was frustrating but Penney was thrilled to be in these heat races getting more experience.

For years Lyle's routine was to eat a good meal four to five hours before the race. (He found he could not withstand the Gs on an empty stomach. Conversely, a full stomach made him a little sluggish.) Then he spent a couple hours relaxing in the pits, talking to visitors, fans, and crew members. But two to three hours before take-off Lyle disappeared.

"I went back to an old habit I had during my boxing days – a good meal followed by a nap," he explained. " Flying the *Rare Bear* is a lot like getting into a boxing match; it's a big physical drain in a close race. We're out to win so I need my energy. I'm kind of a napper anyway. When my energy runs out I'm no good until I get a catnap"

While he sequestered himself, Lyle thought about the upcoming race. "When I'm planning I'm thinking more tactical than mechanical. Tactics are not all that complicated – fly fast, turn left. The tactics develop as response to specific situations. All that is based on previous experience. In recent years the start of the race is all-important. When you are coming down the slot it's important that you have everything set up with the power and hope nobody's turning into you or diving under you. I don't really think very much about specifics, just deal with situations as they come up. It's instinctive. No micro-reviewing."

On Saturday *Rare Bear* came in three seconds ahead of *Strega* to win and even the competition for this year at one heat race each. Everybody in the pits was waiting for the Sunday Gold race. It would be an all-out, no horses spared shoot-out!

The tension and anticipation continued to build in the Unlimited pits Sunday afternoon. Warm weather, clear skies, and healthy airplanes promised one heck of a race. The pairings listed Lyle in pole position, Destefani second, Holm third, Dennis Sanders in *Dreadnought* fourth, Bill Rheinschild in *Risky Business* fifth, John Maloney in *Super Corsair* sixth, Delbert Williams in *Pegasus* seventh, Bob Yancey in *Perestroika* eighth, and Howard Pardue in the Hawker ISS Sea Fury in ninth position.

Fans did not leave early Sunday to beat the traffic; air race crews were jostling for position at the flight line, and the concession stands were deserted of customers as the racers roared onto the course. Lyle pushed the throttle forward and shot out front as they heard the familiar words, "Gentlemen, you have a race." And it was indeed a race.

Lap after lap Lyle smoothly banked *Rare Bear* around the pylons. Beneath him officials stood next to the pylon, looking intently upwards as the planes flashed over them. They were there to verify the pilot did not drift inside a pylon to shave a precious second off his time.

Sharon Coates, race announcer Sandy Sanders' assistant, timed the laps to keep him informed of speeds.

LAP MPH

1.	479.86
2.	478.46
3.	480.42
4.	483.75
5.	481.76
6.	477.70 [*]
7.	483.25
8.	487.68

AVERAGE: 481.61

◆THE DROP IN SPEED ON LAP SIX OCCURRED AS SHELTON LAPPED THE SLOWER AIRCRAFT IN THE RACE.

DESTEFANI AND HOLM WERE CLOSE BEHIND AT THE FINISH
WITH AVERAGE SPEEDS OF 478.680 MPH AND 478.140 MPH
RESPECTIVELY.

Lyle not only won his fourth straight Reno Unlimited championship he shattered his previous year's speed record by 12.998 mph and advanced his total Reno Unlimited victories to six.

After the race, the winner was parked proudly in front of the grandstands. Jack DeBoer and Lyle were beaming when the crew and dozens of spectators surrounded them in front of *Rare Bear*. Their euphoria lasted through the evening at the air race banquet as they took the stage to accept the trophy and the crew jumped and shouted "Four-peat! Four-peat". Lyle's wife, Joyce, shed happy tears as she stepped beside him to give him a victory kiss.

Winning team, Lyle and Jack DeBoer, 1991.
H. Rourk

"This crew has been through a lot and worked their tails off. It's a great win for them...and for me too," said Lyle. "They deserve the credit. *Rare Bear* never performed better."

Could they do it again next year? Would the brutal hours on the engine, accumulated over the past four years, expose unpredictable problems? They would think about it tomorrow. This night was for celebrating.

On September 25, 1991, John Sandberg was killed while ferrying *Tsunami* back to its home hangar in Minneapolis, Minnesota. He crashed about one mile from the end of the runway of Pierre, South Dakota airport. Witnesses said he appeared to be approaching the runway for a landing when the plane rolled over and went straight down. Sandberg was killed on impact. *Tsunami* was destroyed. It was another significant loss to the sport of air racing and a sober end to the year for the air racing community.

20

Green Was Not a Lucky Color

Carl Friend, long time *Rare Bear* crew member, died of a brain tumor in January, 1992. Friend's innovative ideas resulted in many of the modifications that led to the super speeds the Bearcat achieved. In a message to the crew in June Lyle declared, "This year I would like to dedicate the race effort to Carl. He always put in 200% effort on the *Bear*. He spent hundreds of hours per year for many years running calculations and defining and designing mods, trying to improve our speed – and that he did!"

Some ignition problems appeared during the 1991 Gold race that Lyle felt had to be corrected before attempting a ferry flight back to Van Nuys. After the Christmas-New Year holidays several crew members commuted to Stead to do the work. A sobering look at the team's finances disclosed expenditures for 1991 exceeded income by over $4,000. Prize money received was $54,000; cash from sponsors was $32,000; cash from Lyle's savings was $20,000. The crew was paid zero for over 6,000 hours work during the year, plus that performed at Reno during race week. Los Angeles County assessed $18,000 in property taxes on the airplane due March 1. The tax was based on their valuation of the aircraft of one million dollars.

Lyle bitterly exclaimed, "If they can come up with a buyer who will pay me that much, I'll take it."

The $86,000 he had received from prize money and sponsorship did not cover the insurance, hangar rent, repair parts, supplies, taxes, and crew expenses. He had already used $20,000 from his savings. When his sponsorship agreement was up for renewal he and DeBoer could not agree on new terms.

Lyle's worries increased in February when he was ticketed for a DUI while driving home one evening after dinner with friends. His pilot's license could be in jeopardy.

It was not until May, 1992, that Lyle was able to fly *Rare Bear* back to Van Nuys and the crew start basic maintenance. They needed to thoroughly inspect all engine parts that had been pushed to extremes over the last four years. Small problems had appeared, and were quickly repaired at the race site. It was not the problems they knew about that worried them. Inspection of the propeller found very little wear. Some cylinders were changed, oil leaks chased down, and the exhaust reworked. Prewitt remanufactured the flame panels at his new shop in Van Nuys. Some wiring and regulators were relocated. Shell Oil helped out by delivering 110 gallons of their new multi-viscosity oil to be used in flight tests.

During the summer a new sponsor, Harry Thomason of Thomason Aircraft Corporation in Van Nuys, was recruited by Bill Noctor. When *Rare Bear* arrived in Reno in September, 1992, it wore a radical new white with green paint scheme (Thomason's corporate colors). One superstitious crew member was apprehensive about using green, "an unlucky color in racing," he moaned. When the *Bear* posted a new record qualifying speed of 482.892 mph his concerns seemed premature. Maybe not! Later in the day Penney took the *Bear* up to cruise a few laps and heard a sudden pop from the engine. He made an emergency landing with lots more than the usual oil dripping down the sides. The crew now wondered if the color green really was a jinx. Racers are a superstitious bunch at times.

As per the Unlimited schedule the top five qualifiers did not race on Thursday. This gave the Bearcat crew time to inspect the damage from Tuesday's engine failure. They found the #12 cylinder had a hole in it. Most agonizing was the presence of metal particles in the oil screen. No telling how much damage was inside the rest of the engine. With the time they had before the Friday race they could only replace the cylinder and piston. Runups appeared normal so the Bear stayed in the lineup.

Rare Bear was not the only airplane having troubles. About forty-five minutes remained before the deadline when Brickert finally qualified the *Pond Racer* at a disappointing 358.625 mph. When setting up for his landing he asked for fire trucks to be on alert because he had a leak. He believed it was water coolant but precautions were in order. The situation became serious when he and Lloyd Hamilton appeared to be on course for a head-on collision on the runway. With Brickert coming in eastward Hamilton was already rolling westward down the runway on his landing. Brickert was able to pull up, realign himself with one of the emergency runways, and landed safely. He continued having engine problems but did place second in the Bronze race.

After air show acts and racing ended on Friday *Rare Bear* crew assembled on the taxiway to watch as Jane Friend and her family went aloft in Mike Bogue's B-23 *Dragon* to fulfill Carl Friend's last wish; he wanted his ashes scattered at the Reno air-race course. Airport and RARA authorities gave permission to do so. The Bearcat crew stood at attention along the runway as the B-23, piloted by Denny Ghiringhelli, flew past them while Somers Blackman scattered Carl's ashes over the race course.

Rare Bear's problems continued on Saturday. Try as he might, Lyle was unable to catch Destefani in their heat race. Lyle's concerns mounted. The crew did not know the exact damage they faced and what could happen on Sunday when Lyle would push the throttle to the limit. They found out on the fifth lap. Destefani was about two seconds in front of the *Bear* when it belched smoke. Lyle declared a mayday, then landed on one of the emergency runways, ending with a ground loop. Back in the pits the crew's inspection found the front master rod had broken sending two pistons through the sides of the cylinders. The ground loop caused no air frame damage. Destefani went on to win the Gold race with the speed of 450.835 mph. The *Bear* was towed to the RARA's hangar where it sat for the next three months. Their winning streak ended at four.

In October crew members removed the engine and propeller for transport to Van Nuys. When they took the engine apart they found a lot of damage; metal pieces were found in odd places as they stripped off the parts. This engine was junk. In past years when the engine and fuselage were in separate locations the crew was frustrated. They were unable to coordinate work on the systems as needed. After several meetings with crew members Lyle decided to disassemble the aircraft and truck it to Van Nuys. Work began with different members coming to Reno as they were able. Bill Coulter took a week's vacation to work on it. Bill Hickle flew in for several weekends to work; local crew members were willing assistants. Of immeasurable help were Al Redick's Aviation Classics Ltd. mechanics .

Rare Bear was not easy to tear apart. Hickle had helped modify the wreck and build an air racer out of it in 1969. Now he was tearing it apart and involved in engineering and reconstructing the airplane so it could fly once again. He recalled that they originally put in over 570 rivets to hold the two main sections together. Now he struggled to remove all of them in a very cold hangar in the middle of winter. Once the rivets were removed the tail section was anchored at one end while the wing/cockpit section was pulled the opposite direction using a huge forklift driven by Juan Redick. It was late afternoon, cold, with darkening skies as the crew watched anxiously for the two sections to separate. They did not budge a fraction of an inch. Finally Dell Rourk and Hickle wedged themselves into the hell-hole to locate the problem. As Rourk held a flashlight Hickle discovered four large bolts were holding the airplane sections together. There was almost no room to maneuver or breathe as Hickle wrestled those four bolts loose. It was after 9:00 p.m. when Redick and his monster forklift tugged on the chains once more and cleanly separated the two sections. The wing/cockpit section was loaded onto a flatbed truck; the fuselage was loaded onto a stake truck. One February day in 1993, following a heavy snowstorm that closed two of the major routes into and out of Reno for two days, volunteers Norm Willick and John Mackamon drove two trucks loaded with what looked sadly like a wrecked airplane away from Stead. When it got to Van Nuys the re-assembling of *Rare Bear* began.

Lyle left Vancouver, British Columbia, on May 22, 1993, aboard the cruise ship *Westerdan* of the Holland America Line as host/speaker for a seven-day cruise designed for air race fans. Race pilot Skip Holm and Destefani's crew chief, Bill Kerchenfaut, shared the host duties. They showed slides, video tapes and answered questions for fifty-five air race fans aboard to learn more about air racing. Besides learning first-hand about the world's fastest motor sport they enjoyed cruising the waters off the Alaskan coast. They made stops in Ketchikan, Juneau, and Sitka; enjoyed a ride in an Otter to one of Alaska's beautiful inland lakes; thrilled to sightings of whales, dolphins, and many sea birds; and experienced a hike on a glacier. Lyle was thrilled to visit Alaska again. He enjoyed speaking about his favorite subject – air racing – and was well-received by the passengers on board who wanted to hear about it from the champions.

Rare Bear did not make it to Reno in 1993, but Lyle did. He watched in dismay as the Unlimited Division lost veteran pilot Rick Brickert and the second custom built air racer. It was late afternoon Wednesday and the deadline was less than an hour away when Brickert took off intending to qualify *Pond Racer*. He completed one lap on the course, then radioed his intention to qualify on the next lap. As he increased power he suddenly pulled up near pylon 4 and radioed a mayday. The right engine was trailing smoke as he headed toward the main runway. On the downwind leg his right engine stopped. He lowered the landing gear when he turned on base leg but at the last minute he headed for the dry lake bed beyond the end of the runway. The tower lost radio contact as he dropped from sight down into the lake bed area. Witnesses said he retracted the gear and bellied into the sand and sagebrush out there, bouncing one or two times before bursting into flames. Firefighters were unable to suppress the fire in time to save the 38-year old pilot. The Unlimited Division paid tribute to Brickert with missing man formations Thursday evening and Sunday afternoon before the Gold race.

Destefani flew *Strega* to their third Reno Gold race win on Sunday with the winning speed of 455.380 mph.

In October it was officially announced the first Phoenix 500 Air Race would be held at the former Williams Air Force Base near Chandler, Arizona, in May, 1994. The field was now called Williams Gateway Airport. Lyle could not commit to bring *Rare Bear* to Phoenix without a sponsor. Work was slowly progressing on rebuilding the Bearcat engine as Lyle found funds for new parts. Bill Jones, of Aircraft Cylinder and Turbine, bought and installed a much-needed new canopy. In December Ben Visser of Shell Development Company stepped in and discussions began about sponsorship money in return for testing a new Shell

25W/50 oil in the engine. The sagging spirits of the crew soared. They were sure they could get *Rare Bear* ready in time for Phoenix. Airline and hotel reservations were made. Work schedules were accelerated. A few bars of "By the time we get to Phoenix we'll be ready," were heard now and then and always somebody shouted, "We'll be winning!"

But 1994 held some unexpected challenges for *Rare Bear* and the crew before they would race again.

Rare Bear cockpit, 1992
Shelton Collection

21

PHOENIX, OSHKOSH, RENO

Southern California experienced a major earthquake early in the morning of January 17, 1994. It could have dealt Lyle and the *Rare Bear Air Racing Team* a mortal blow. The epicenter of the 6.6 quake was about six miles from the hangar in Van Nuys where the *Bear* was sitting up on jacks with the main gear barely touching the floor. After the quake the hangar floor was littered with tools, nuts and bolts.. The only damage to the plane was near the tail section where a tool fell out of a cabinet and bounced pretty hard.. Several other hangars at the field suffered extensive damage together with the aircraft they housed. According to crew member Gordon Symon, when he arrived at the hangar less than hour later he asked *Bear* how it felt. *Bear* shrugged and replied, "OK, I thought it was just another rough landing." *Bear* might be over forty and rather fat; certainly it was fast; but it was also durable.

Lyle was grounded while he appealed a DUI conviction. Penney agreed to supervise the work needed before the Bearcat would be ready for an upcoming race at Phoenix, Arizona in March, 1994. Aircraft Cylinder and Turbine and Aeroshell became co-sponsors, with Shell providing $35,000 to keep the repair work going. After the quake cleanup was done the crew immediately went back to installing the new canopy and the never ending work on the engine. Lyle approved some changes in the cockpit instrument display to help the pilots quickly read key instruments during a race. Engine instruments that were more critical were displayed on the left side, "because you are always in a left turn---as you are looking out your eyeballs keep looking left."

Penney was excited and enthusiastic about the project. The Bearcat, however, was no more cooperative for Penney than it had been for Lyle. With the usual flair for the dramatic it posed one problem after another before Penney was able to get it into the air again. A daily journal he kept logged the progress of the work and some of the frustrations they faced:

"*Monday, 14 March:* Crew works all day long, into the night. Flight test at Mojave now out of the question. Need to fly locally Tuesday AM or call if all off. Alternators still not hooked up, cowling at the painters, radios nowhere to be found, canopy not installed. Estimate: No flying Tuesday. Crew dead tired, works into the night.

Tuesday, 15 March: Absolutely need to test fly this afternoon or call it off! Electrical system being completed. Radios being installed. Helped install canopy. Cowling arrived but didn't fit! Start grinding fairings. *Tuesday evening:* Engine run. Still no rpm gauge. Engine cuts out and backfired when cycling #1 mag in "R" and "off" positions. Miswiring problem fixed (we thought). *Tuessday L.A.T.E. evening:* No test flight today. Will be forced to test fly tomorrow AM before launching for PHX. (This is stupid. Violating everything I've learned about safety and common sense). Crew exhausted...they work into the night.

Wednesday, 16 March, 0500 hours: Aircraft start normal, waiting at runway for tower to open at 7:00 a.m. First flight, 20 minutes. RPM gauge busted, *0800 hours:* Launch for PHX with a turbo jet in the chase. Leave chase in the dust! He requests I do a 360 turn so he can catch up. Negative! I throttle back. Jet catches up 1/3 the way to PHX. '*Rare Bear* with chase on initial for pattern at Williams' elicits stone dead silence from every soul on the ramp. Deadline for registration is 1100 hours. Land at 1015. Forty-five minutes to spare. No sweat"

Heat races over the next three days gave the pilots opportunities to become familiar with the course and plan their strategy for the Gold Race on Sunday. Spectators and crews watched in horror on Saturday as Planes of Fame *Super Corsair*, piloted by Kevin Eldriddge . flew about 700 feet above the far end of the course streaming bright orange flames and thick black smoke behind him. They could not hear John Maloney's frantic radio transmission to Eldgridge to bail out, they could only stand paralyzed and helpless and pray for the pilot. As the *Super Corsair* rolled over and nosed downward smoke kept many from seeing Eldridge as he exited the plane and parachuted to the ground. He survived his injuries and was back flying – and racing again.

On Sunday Penney flew the eight lap race at Phoenix to take his first ever checkered flag flying *Rare Bear* to an average speed of 434.158 mph.

Paul Poberezny invited Lyle to bring *Rare Bear* to Oshkosh for the annual EAA Fly-In in late July, 1994. It was a new experience for Penney to ferry the temperamental *Rare Bear* half-way across the continent. It made the short flight from Los Angeles to Phoenix in March look like a Sunday outing.

Aeroshell 15W-50W oil, sponsor for the flight, set up a full schedule of personal appearances and talks for Lyle while Penney flew the demonstration flights.

The Reno Air Races in September , 1994 were the most difficult for the grounded champion. He walked around the pits, chatting with old friends and fans, while Penney was setting new speed records in the air. He was relieved when this miserable year ended.

Ida Mae Shelton died unexpectedly of heart failure in February, 1995. This was a devastating loss for Lyle. One of twelve children, Mrs. Shelton lived all her life in the Brownfield, Texas area. Many of her sisters and brothers had lived in and raised their families in or near this quiet West Texas town. They were Lyle's Brownfield cheering section. This was where he came to forget the problems of air racing and catch up on the comings and goings of life-long friends, aunts, uncles, and cousins. Mrs. Shelton was very proud of Lyle's accomplishments; she had a room at her home filled with his trophies and memorabilia. During the 3-Km speed run she had driven to Las Vegas to watch Lyle attempt a record she knew he wanted for so many years. It was hot and dusty at the field but Mrs. Shelton was there every day sitting quietly in the shade of the old hangar as the crew bustled around the airplane. She calmly watched as her son risked his life for speed. She was a gentle, gracious lady with a warm smile who would be greatly missed by everyone, especially by her only son.

Penney and Lyle were not anxious to participate in the Phoenix Air Race in 1996. They had not been paid the prize money they had earned for the past two years. When the Phoenix promoters agreed to payment of $22,000 on what they owed, Penney agreed to bring *Rare Bear* to the event to "give the *Rare Bear Air Racing Team* exposure". It also gave the crew the opportunity to work some more on the engine. Flying was limited to demo races.

The engine was tweaked and tuned when Lyle climbed into the cockpit for a test flight at Reno in September, 1996. After trial runs early in the week, Lyle called the crew together to tell them he was turning the cockpit over to Penney for the rest of the race week. He admitted he was out of practice and not comfortable with the changes to *Rare Bear*. It was one of the hardest decisions he had made during his years of air racing.

A strong cold front descended on Stead on Sunday as Penney and the Unlimiteds climbed out into the turbulent air. On the second lap Penney told the crew over the radio that he had heard something go and he was coming in. As he watched, Lyle was relieved to see *Rare Bear* touch down safely. The entire left side, from cowling to tail feathers, was covered in black oil.

Once again Lyle faced a broken engine, long hours of exhausted mechanics trying to find the problem, and more money for needed repair parts. He asked himself if he really wanted to do this. Once again the answer was "Yes".

It was the end of April, 1997, before the rebuilt engine was ready for test stand runups. On May 21st the crew said everything looked good and Lyle made the first test hop. Penney took *Rare Bear* up for a high-powered test fight in mid-June. When Lyle was ferrying the Bearcat to Reno for the races in September, 1997 he noticed fuel dripping from the fuel gauge onto his leg. After the gauge was repaired he found he had handling problems when he was pulling four to five "gs". The nose of the *Bear* was coming up and forcing him to push forward on the stick to avoid an out-of-control pitch-up. On Sunday, near the end of the third lap, an exhaust stack broke; the hot air from the stack directed against the inside of the cowling. It burned a hole in the cowling right ahead of the leading edge of the wing which has a carburetor intake duct. As it burned shreds of aluminum flew back into the carburetor intake duct and sucked through the engine, knocked out plugs and damaged at least one cylinder, causing the engine to run rough. Lyle pulled up to about 500 feet to get a little room in case things got more serious, but he did not want a DNF for the race.

"When I finished the race I was running 2200-2300hp. After crossing the finish line I immediately declared a mayday and made an emergency landing." He finished third at 423.809 mph after a 16-second penalty for a pylon cut on lap 3, about the time the stack blew.

This was the last time Lyle Shelton raced *Rare Bear*.

22

Motorsports Hall of Fame

On June 11, 1999 Lyle Shelton was inducted into the Motorsports Hall of Fame in a ceremony held at the State Theater in Novi, Michigan, a suburb of Detroit.

Family and friends were in the audience as Lyle, formally dressed in a tuxedo and black tie, joined George Follmer (Trans-Am champion), C.J. "Pappy" Hart (drag race champion), Bret Markel (motocycle champion) and Bill Seebold Jr (boat race champion) in the ceremony that placed them in the Motorsports Hall of Fame. Also inducted, but not present, were Henry Miller (Indy car designer), Jimmy Bryant (Indy car racer), Tim flock (NASCAR driver), and Frank Kurtis, (Indy car designer/builder).

As is to be expected, champions from the various categories of auto racing dominate the museum. You can find tributes to Mario Andretti, Dave Garlitrz, Shirley Muldowney and A.J. Foyt, along with many more, in these rooms.

Legendary air racers also have their space in this motor sports mecca. Glenn Curtiss, winner of the first air race held in France in 1909, is there. So are Jimmy Doolittle and Roscoe Turner, both pioneer air racers. Only a handful of men have been selected to join these motor sports champions

From the beginning of his racing career in 1965 Lyle's love of flying and his quest for faster speeds propelled him to new records and into the winner's circle at numerous races. He was proud to be included in the company of so many legendary speed seekers.

Lyle inducted into Motorsports Hall of Fame, 1999.
Courtesy of Motorsports Hall of Fame

EPILOGUE

Although Lyle Shelton retired from air racing after the 1997 Reno Air Race, *Rare Bear* did not. Engine problems kept it on the ground in 1998, 2000, and 2002. The September 11, 2001 terrorist attack in New York City occurred at the beginning of the 2001 Reno Air Races; all planes were grounded and racing was cancelled. Matt Jackson flew the Bear in 1999; He qualified but was out with engine problems after the first heat race. John Penney flew the Reno races in 2003, 2004, and 2005. He scored two Gold race wins and one second place finish. Ron Buccarelli qualified *Rare Bear* at Reno in 2006; however, engine problems kept it from actually racing.

In November, 2006, while *Rare Bear* rested quietly in a hangar at Stead Field, Lyle reluctantly accepted Rod Lewis's offer to buy the legendary aircraft he had rescued, rebuilt, and raced to glory over the past thirty years.

Rare Bear will fly again!

Lyle Shelton's NAA/FAI Records

February 6, 1972   Time-to-Climb record, Zero to 3,000
                            meters in 91.9 seconds
                            Thermal Airport near Indio, California
                            Grumman F8F-2 Bearcat

August 21, 1989   Km piston engine propeller driven aircraft
                            world speed record, 528.33   mph, Las
                            Vegas Airport, New Mexico
                            Grumman F8F-2 Bearcat

August 19, 1976   Wichita, Kansas to Amarillo, Texas,
                            292 miles, 32 minutes 44 seconds
                            Average speed 534.96 miles mph
                            TWA Boeing 727-231

December 30, 1976   Phoenix Sky Harbor International Airport
                            to Amarillo, Texas,
                            598 miles, One hour 1 minute 18 seconds,
                            Average speed 586.27 mph
                            TWA Boeing 727-231A

December 23, 1986   St. Louis, Missouri to Colorado Springs,
                            Colorado.
                            Average speed 429.51 mph
                            TWA Boeing 727

December 26, 1986   St. Louis, Missouri to Salt Lake City,
                            Utah.
                            Average speed 446.96 mph
                            TWA Boeing 727

June 3, 1988   St. Louis, Missouri to Dallas, Texas
                            Average speed 480.07 mph
                            TWA DC-9-31

February 14, 1989	Las Vegas, Nevada to St. Louis, Missouri
	Average speed 595.72 mph, 2 hours 18 minutes
	TWA MD 80
September 8, 1991	Mojave, California to Reno, Nevada.
	Average speed 384.54 mp
	Grumman F8F-2 Bearcat

ENGINE:

3400 hp (2535 KW) Wright R-3350-18EA-1 Turbo-Compound radial piston engine.	Used on Douglas DC-7. Page 135 *Encyclopedia of The World's Commercial and Private Aircraft.*
3250 hp Wright R-3350-DA-3 Turbo-Compound 18 cylinder radial engine.	Used on L-1049 Super Constellation, Lockheed Page 171
3250 hp Wright R-3350-18DA-2 Turbo-Compound engine	Used on Douglas DC-7 Page 188
3400 hp Wright R-3350-EA-2 Turbo Compound 18-cylinder radial engine	Used on L-1648A Starliner, Lockheed Page 192 *The Illustrated Encyclopedia of Propeller Airliners*

After carefully studying 18 months of information concerning air combat from the carriers Grumman designed the F8F, a totally new fighter that was smaller and 2,000 lbs lighter than the F6F and one of the most compact machines of its time, despite being powered by the same chunky and powerful R-2800 Double Wasp engine. The engine turned a big four-blade propeller, and the result was a fighter that had few rivals for speed, quick takeoff, rate and angle of climb, and all-round combat maneuverability. Two prototypes were ordered on 11/27/43, and the first flew on 8/31/44. The F8F could be called an engine with a saddle on it. The center of gravity was eight inches ahead of the engine firewall. The top of the aircraft's one-piece wing formed the floor of the cockpit, and the pilot sat on a sheet of metal attached to a structure above the wing. By adding his own personalized cushion, the pilot raised himself high enough to see out of the cockpit. A big man had to sit a little sideways to fit between the cockpit side rails. Grumman built 365 F8F-2s with a taller fin.

PAGE 48-51

GRUMMAN: SIXTY YEARS OF EXCELLENCE BY BILL GUNSTON

BIBLIOGRAPHY

Dresselhaus, Donald E., *I Never Flew Alone*, Star Printing, Evansville, WI, 1968

Berliner, Don, *World Wide Directory of Air Racing Airplanes, Vol. 1*, Aviation Publishing Co., 1997

Curtiss-Wright, *Handbook Overhaul Instructions, Navy Models R-3350W, Aircraft Engines*, 8/30/68, Changed 7/15/72

Gunston, Bill, *Sixty Years of Excellence*, Orion Books (Crown Publishers, Inc.) New York, 1988

Gunston, Bill, *Illustrated Encyclopedia of Propeller Airliners*, Phoebus Publ. Co., London, Eng., 1980

Heywood, John B., *Internal Combustion Engine Fundamentals*, McGraw-Hill Book Co., 1988

Hull, Robert, *September Champions*, Stackpole Books, Harrisburg, PA, 1979

Huntington, Roger, *Thompson Trophy Racers*, Motorbooks International, Osceola, WI, 1989

Jerram, Mike, *Reno 2*, Osprey Publishing, London, Eng., 1986

Kaufman, Robert, 'Yogi', *City at Sea*, Aircraft Carriers USA, 1995

Kinert, Reed, *Racing Planes and Air Racers*, Aero Publishers, Fallbrook, CA. 1970

Larsen, Jim, *Directory of Unlimited Class Pylon Air Racers*, American Air Museum, Kirkland, WA 1971

Maloney, Edward T., *Grumman F8F Bearcat*, Col. 20, Aero Publishers, Inc., Fallbrook, CA 1969

Matthews, Birch, *Wet Wings and Drop Tanks*, Schiffer Publishing, Ltd, Atglen, PA 1993

Matthews, Birch, *Race With the Wind, How Air Racing Acvanced Aviation*, MBI Publ. Co., Osceola, WI 2001

Matthews, Birch and Dustin Carter, *Mustang, The Racing Thoroughbred*, Schiffer Publ, Ltd, 1993

Mendenhall, Charles A., *The Air Racer*, Specialty Press Publishers & Wholesalers, Inc., North Branch, MN 1979

O'Leary, Michael, *U.S. Naval Fighters of WW II*, Blandford Press, Poole, Dorset, 1980

O'Neil, Paul, *Barnstormers & Speed Kings*, Time-Life Books, Alexandria, VA 1981

Rashke, Richard, *Stormy Genius, the Life of Aviation's Maverick, Bill Lear*, Houghton Mifflin Co., Boston, 1985

Scrivner, Charles, *F8F Bearcat in Action*, Squadron Signal Publications, Carrolton, TX, 1990

Smith, Herschel, *Aircraft Piston Engines, Manly Baltzer to Continental Tiara*, McGraw-Hill Book Co., 1981

Tegler, *John Gentlemen, You Have a Race*, Wings Publishing Co., Severna, MD, 1984

Thruelsen, Richard, *The Grumman Story*, Praeger Publishers, New York, 1976

White, Graham, *Allied Aircraft Piston Engines of WW II*, Society of Auromotive Engineers, Inc., Warrendale, PA, 1945

World & United States Aviation & Space Records, (as of 12/31/95), National Aeronautic Association of the USA, Arlington, VA, 1996

PERIODICALS:

Arizona Flyways, *Reno Air Races*, July, 1995, p. 19

Coholic, Suzanne, *Lyle & The Bear*, Air Racing, Vol. 2, 1993 (Air Classics Special)

Downie, Don, *The Fury of Mike Carroll*, Air Progress, September, 1967

Fey, Tom, *Unlimited Nuts and Bolts*, Speed, Props and Pylons, May/June, 1993

Matthews, Birch, *Rare Bear, A Gold Race Record at Reno*, American Aviation Historical Journal, Vol 36, #2, Summer, 1991

Richard, John L., *Reno Notebook*, Air Progress, January, 1992, PPG 47-51

Rourk, Dell, *Fly Fast*, Reno Air Race Association Program, September, 1994

Rourk, Dell, *Lyle Shelton and Rare Bear*, Finish Line, Vol 3, #4, December 1996; Vol 4, #1, March 1997

Rourk, Dell, *Air Racing*, pp. 81-85, Sports Encyclopedia of America, Academic Internationsl Press, Gulf Breeze, FL, Feb. 1987

Sandberg, Sharon, *Rare Bear Camp News*, Speed, Props and Pylons, Issue #3, 1998

Tegler, John, *Tiger Wins with a Bear Behind*, Airshow International, Spring, 1993

Ward, Dave, *A Man & A Bear; The Great Blayde*, Bear Facts newsletter, 1989

Weir, Marc, *Tech File*, Bear Facts Newsletter, March 1998

NEWSPAPERS:

Barber, Phil, *Top Guns of Reno Air Races Threaten Boycott*, Reno Gazette-Journal, 3/30/90

Sneddon, Steve, *Land Speed Record*, Reno Gazette-Journal, 10/24/96

53209002R00119

Made in the USA
San Bernardino, CA
09 September 2017